Jump-Start Your Merchandising Career

JUMP-START YOUR MERCHANDISING CAREER

JUDITH ADKINS-SPEARS

Library of Congress Control Number: 2010919350
ISBN: Hardcover 978-1-4568-4217-8
Softcover 978-1-4568-4216-1
Ebook 978-1-4568-4218-5

To order additional copies of this book, contact:
Xlibris Corporation
1-888-795-4274
www.Xlibris.com
Orders@Xlibris.com
88390

CONTENTS

ACKNOWLEDGEMENTS

I want to dedicate it to my parents, Winston Adkins and Rosenelle Boyd Adkins. They instilled a great love of books, as well as education in me.

Without my husband, Bobby, I would be nothing. I am sorry you come in second behind my parents, but always know you are my steadying rock.

I would also like to thank the following folks who without their knowledge and willingness to share their immeasurable contributions to the content of this book it could never have been written.

- Debbie Owen, my first merchandising supervisor, who with much patience, taught me what I needed to know to start merchandising.
- Pat Brown, one of my merchandising supervisors, who has taught me how to stay calm, cool, and collected in the face of adversity.
- Ray Sola, owner of Volition.com, LLC, a true online friend to merchandisers and mystery shoppers.
- PamInCa, IMSC President, who guided me during the last stages of my book.
- Darnella Bradley who patiently listened to me and then did the first editing job.

CHAPTER 1

Introduction to Merchandising

In This Chapter

❖ What Merchandisers Do
❖ Requirements for the Beginning Merchandiser
❖ Merchandiser's Pay
❖ Merchandiser Role Recap
❖ Choose Mystery Shopping or Merchandising?
❖ Merchandising Paperwork
❖ Merchandising Assignment Availability
❖ Merchandiser Activity Recap

When I first set out to write this book, I consulted most of the store managers with which I had subcontracted. I told them I had checked in various places and could not find a book in publication that showed new merchandisers how to get off the ground and get their feet wet. All of them responded with, "Judy, if anybody can write that book, you can. You have worked in so many different types of stores that you have seen a little bit of everything." Some of them even admitted that at times I had taught them something. I told them that although there was no way to cover anything but the basics in one book, I wanted to make it as complete as possible. Therefore, if you have a question regarding any merchandising project or concept, then I cannot stress enough that you should contact your supervisor.

I wrote this book with new, or fairly new, merchandisers in mind. Hopefully, this information will help them get a head start in their chosen career. I have never written a book before. I have not even written a manual. I tackled this job the same way I did research papers in school. I used everything I had learned from every company I had worked for as a merchandiser or mystery shopper. I then attempted to roll it all into one piece of meaningful information that would make sense to someone else. Therefore, I am writing this in a conversational tone instead of in terminology everyone will need to look up in dictionaries. I truly admire the ladies who have come before me, paving the way for this book. They have made it possible for me to realize my ambition of presenting all that I have learned over the years to help the ones coming after me. I am including an in-depth glossary at the end for those who need or just want the terminology. When I started out, I knew *nothing*!

When I was hired for my first merchandising job, I called my daughter in Florida, and she went over the planogram with me on the phone. She said, "Mom, you have two bachelor's degrees and a master's degree, you can do this." It was a cosmetic reset with wallpaper. I arrived at the store on time, removed everything from the wall, cleared the pegs, put the product in buggies, and peeled several layers of labels off those pegs. Only one hour had passed, and I was on a roll!

I then proceeded to attempt to put up the wallpaper, which did not fit correctly. I asked the manager what to do, and she had no idea other than to cut it off. So cut it I did. *Then* I put it up; it fit perfectly across, but was too short! I realized I had it turned wrong initially. When I started putting the product up, it was like a treasure hunt. Finally, I put up all the pegs and tags and went from there. The eight-hour reset took two days. (I turned in only eight hours on the payroll.) The manager loved the result! I got six more jobs just like it, but I had learned bushels on that one and did not make the same mistakes twice.

With these confessions in mind, I enthusiastically welcome you to the wide, wild, wonderful world of merchandising! You are about to learn the secrets stores usually keep behind closed Employees Only doors. Before doing this type of work, I had no idea what a merchandiser was or what he/ she did. When I considered how merchandise got on the shelves or what happened when someone picked up an item from one side of the store and laid it down somewhere else, I always assumed that store personnel handled all these tasks.

I started to say, "Handled these merchandising tasks," but at that time, I had no idea they were called merchandising tasks. I just knew that when I went in my favorite store, whatever I was looking for was on the shelf. In the days of smaller, more family-oriented stores, the store employees did all this work. Now, when someone asks me what I do, I reply with, "You know when you go into a store, and you look for your favorite shampoo in its usual place and something else is there? I am one of those people who went in and moved everything around."

Before the large supercenters came into existence, there were plenty of knowledgeable store personnel to take care of both the product's and the shoppers' needs. Most retailers today are looking for ways to save money, and many times, they choose to cut back in store personnel as a way to save. For shoppers, this means a more self-serve attitude as they are usually forced to help themselves. For products, this means less time can be spent on merchandising.

Corporate product headquarters decided they had to get involved or their products were going to suffer. Their solution was to hire a group of people who were dedicated only to product support and known as merchandisers!

What Merchandisers Do

Merchandisers are primarily contracted to work for the products' corporate headquarters. Their job is to ensure the company's products are readily available and aesthetically pleasing to consumers at store level. The principal responsibility of a merchandiser is to visit retail locations in order to merchandise their client's products. Corporate Headquarters is keenly aware of how to sell their products. First, the product must be actively distributed. Second, the presentation of the product must meet intended guidelines. Finally, the product must be promoted properly.

There are excellent cases pointing to the need of a merchandiser. Through periodic visits, merchandisers develop a relationship between Corporate Headquarters and store personnel. This rapport between merchandiser and store employees ensures the products are adequately stocked. For example, when product inventory is low, orders will be placed. Department managers will retain authorized product positions; they also obtain the best product placement for the client and obtain new products for display on the sales floor. It is imperative that a merchandiser develop a relationship at the store level. He/she can also build excitement and enthusiasm for the client's product, solve problems more easily, and promptly follow up on merchandising requests and important issues on the client's behalf.

A merchandiser may work directly for the corporate headquarters, for a manufacturer, for a supplier, or for a vendor. Typically, the contracted work is for a specific merchandising company. A manufacturer, a supplier, or a vendor to merchandise the client's product has contracted this company. The corporate headquarters ultimately pays the merchandiser's wages. With more and more stores cutting back on store personnel, the worth of the merchandiser to the store and the products he/she services has never been more significant.

There are many advantages to working as a merchandiser because it is usually an ongoing dependable job. Because you are working independently, you have no boss hovering over your shoulder! If you are hired as an independent contractor, then you own your own business. Infinite opportunities exist where a merchandiser can increase job offers and enhance his/her reputation. Merchandising work is flexible because you accept or decline work offers. Merchandising projects are usually assigned several weeks in advance; therefore, as a merchandiser, you can easily work jobs into your schedule. There are some occasions where the work will be assigned for a specific date and time, such as for resets. You will have the opportunity for advancement to full-time status as you gain more work experience. In my opinion, I derive great satisfaction when I look at a completed project, and I know I have completed a successful job!

There are also some disadvantages to working as a merchandiser. Merchandising work demands all your attention, so children are not allowed on jobs. Resets can be physically demanding. Most merchandising work is to be performed Monday through Friday. Some jobs start before the store is open to customers—you may be there before most employees. Other jobs begin after early customers arrive and continue during midmorning hours. This is either good or bad depending on your particular circumstances.

Requirements for the Beginning Merchandiser

The requirements for beginning merchandisers vary from company to company and job to job. The requirements for the jobs are the most important because individual companies usually, and I use that term "loosely," zoom in on one type of merchandising.

If the company mostly does filling coupon holders, placing IRCs (Instant Redeemable Coupons), and putting up graphics, you can usually eliminate the weight-lifting requirement. You also would not have to know how to read a planogram to do these jobs.

For most people who take merchandising assignments, it involves working at medium-size retailers up to the local stores for large chains. These large chains are supermarkets and drugstores, and even mass merchants like *Target*, *Wal-Mart*, or *Linens & Things*.

From the accounts of many merchandisers, the one constant theme is the variety of work that is available. There is never a dull moment for the person who takes a merchandising assignment. And the great thing is, you, the merchandiser, decides which types of merchandising engagements you enjoy most, and go on as many as you like. It will not take you long to discover which assignments suit you best, and those will provide you with a great source of extra income.

I am inserting one job description from one company. I *italicized* items that may not be usual industry standards. I highlighted in **BOLD** items that are usual for most companies.

Position Title: Field Representative

Job Purpose

Under direct supervision within a defined geographic area, the employee will perform timely duties at customer sites to achieve both profitability and service goals in support of company objectives. He/she will travel in a personal vehicle from one customer location to another, along established routes performing audits, merchandising duties, fixture installation, temporary signage placement (Point of Sale or POS or other services at retail/customer sites as required.

Duties and Responsibilities

- The employee will visit stores as requested to conduct work with *hand tools and small electric tools for the assembly and repair of in-store fixtures, remove old fixtures,* **correctly label all fixtures and reset merchandise per planogram**, *safely use tools for the purpose the tools are designed, and wear protective safety glasses.*
- **Conduct store visit to have signage on site or transporting it to site.** This may require tools and the calculation and **application of correct price stickers.**
- **Install Point of Sale (POS) signage accurately and quickly as required by work order, calculate and apply correct price stickers, and instruct management on correct procedure to change pricing.**
- **Reset Planogram (POG), read planogram and install new tags, move merchandise to match new planogram, and leave store clean and organized when completed.**
- *Maintain all fixtures, order parts as needed, use power tools and supplies to repair,* and **clean fixtures when necessary.** Must have the following tools: *drill, drill bit set,* **hammer, screwdriver set, pliers, plastic scraper,** *small hacksaw,* **tape measure, some type of cleaner (e.g., Goo Gone). Should carry a lanyard with name.**
- **Must have daily access to a computer, printer, and the Internet in order to report completed work, download work schedules, print planograms, directions, and company information.**

Minimum Qualifications

Knowledge

Requires a high school diploma, GED, or equivalent. **Must be computer literate and able to use word-processing, spreadsheets and Windows-based applications to obtain, download and print work schedules, planograms and company information.** Must be knowledgeable about the product and reporting processes and systems.

Experience

Requires a minimum of one year of experience in Consumer Product Group product merchandising or similar field representative or retail experience.

Training/Certification

Will be trained and *certified on all aspects of the* position. *When project certification is required, it may consist of taking and passing one or more comprehensive test(s) computer training information. If project certification is required, the employee will be asked to renew his/her project certification at regular intervals if lack of certification level knowledge is demonstrated.*

Physical Requirements

Ability to lift and carry over 40 lbs. Ability to stand, sit, stoop, bend, walk, reach, squat, kneel, push, pull and drive for long periods of time. Able to climb a ladder and flex the upper and lower body. Must be able to read and write simple statements. Able to analyze, memorize, and conduct and comprehend simple mathematical tasks. Be able to make decisions and have sound judgment.

Work Environment

- **Must be able to work alone and around others. Be able to have verbal and face-to-face contact with others. Must be flexible to work various shifts, work hours, different days of the week, and extended days. Able to travel during daytime or nighttime. Must be able to withstand temperature changes, work under extreme heat, or cold, confined spaces, inside and/or outside, and around dirt or dust.**
- **Employee travels to various retail/customer sites where the customer stocks and sells merchandise.** *Reasonable mileage reimbursement is paid as well as hourly compensation for travel time. The employee's mileage and drive time is frequently audited for accuracy and integrity.* **Each employee is assigned a pre-determined schedule and appropriate route to follow by his or her Team Leader via the web. The employee is expected to travel from one site to the next as per the schedule and report on a timely basis.**
- **Must have access to a personal vehicle for the purpose of commuting between scheduled stores as many as 10-12 per day. Sufficient insurance coverage for said vehicle must be maintained as well as a valid driver's license. Employee must have and keep a clean driving record that meets or exceeds the standards set for drivers in the**

Human Resources Policy Manual. An MVR check will be run prior to employment.

Merchandiser's Pay

The pay depends on many factors. These include your experience, the type of assignment, and the location of the stores. Whether you perform merchandising assignments on a full or part-time basis can also affect your pay scale.

The industry standard for a manufacturer or merchandising company is to pay an hourly wage. This pay rate ranges from $8-$9 per hour to upward of $14-$25 per hour. Or a company may choose to pay a flat rate for the job, which could be from $8-$45 per job.

While mystery shoppers are not paid for mileage, merchandisers often are. That is why I will usually schedule one or more mystery shops along the route or near my merchandising assignments so that I am paid mileage for the trip and still get the best of both worlds. Now, I do not do this if I am being paid drive time or if I subtract the difference off and do not charge the merchandising company for the drive time or if there are any extra miles involved.

The best-scheduled day could start with a mystery shop at a local fast-food restaurant (breakfast paid for and one to go) followed by a service station shop ($5 in gas). Now it is on to the merchandising jobs. There are several on the list for the day. I always go to the farthest away from home to start. That way, if I do not finish, I do not have as far to go back. I visit one drugstore and one convenience store ($30). Same work in the next town ($30). Mystery shop at a fast-food restaurant (lunch paid for and one to go) followed by another service station and more gas ($5). In the next town are one department store, two drugstores, and two convenience stores ($69). I am almost done for the day. Just two more small towns each with a drugstore and a convenience store (total $60). Let us total the day. I had breakfast, lunch, and one of each in a cooler to take home plus the shop fee. Service station shops provided me with $10 in gas. All the mystery shops were out of state, and the company was getting desperate, value $110. Merchandising work totals $189, **for a grand total of $299.**

Keep in mind I only travel this route every twenty-eight days, so this only happens occasionally. Sometimes it will happen on another route, sometimes not. You have to make it happen.

Remember, I have several years' experience in this business. The companies I work for know they can rely on me. They also know when it is crunch time, and they have shops that have to be done *now*; they can call Judy, and if possible, I will be there. That means I am like the US mail; rain, sleet, snow, or dead of night, I will take the job, if the money is right.

All it takes is doing a good job, being reliable and flexible to turn merchandising assignments into very regular work. Again, you will be in control of your own work schedule, within dates and time ranges that the merchandising company determines.

Merchandiser Role Recap

Be Organized

Have all your information, instructions, call reports, forms, POGs, equipment, etc., ready prior to going to the store. Review the in-store objectives and priorities prior to entering the store. It is a good idea to do this before you leave home. This is because if you find you are missing paperwork, it is not too late to print it out. Check any notes you may have taken from the previous service call to this store.

If you have multiple stores to visit, make sure you have planned the most efficient route. Make sure you have directions to each store prior to starting the day.

Be Courteous

Do not take the prime parking spot in front of the store. Be sure to leave the premium spaces for the store customers.

Communicate

If the store requires you to sign in, do so. Greet the store personnel.

Clean Up

Clean up the area of the store you were working in. Do not leave anything behind.

Be Professional

Always conduct yourself in a professional, customer-driven manner.

A side benefit of this regular work is that the company may want to hire you as an employee and, possibly, make you eligible for health benefits. In contrast to mystery shoppers, who are usually independent contractors, this can be a great additional reason for getting into regular merchandising work.

Choose Mystery Shopping or Merchandising?

Why not do both? In a way, they are two sides of the same coin. On one side, you are visiting a retail establishment to check out how well they are selling products and providing services. On the other side, you are organizing a part of that retail establishment to appeal to consumers and to encourage their purchase of the products assigned to handle. So really, mystery shopping and merchandising are the ideal balancing assignments that will give you the maximum amount of perspective for each side. Also, you are often reimbursed for mileage as a merchandiser, and this can help if you combine your merchandising jobs with your mystery shops!

Companies and schedulers, who are hiring for both sides, love to see shoppers who have experience in each field. This makes you, to their eyes, a more well-rounded and perceptive shopper and merchandiser. Even better, from your perspective, mystery shopping and merchandising are a great complement in terms of your schedule. While both are flexible, the merchandising will be very regular, and the mystery shopping can fill in the gaps.

Another consideration is that merchandising tends to be more activity related and physical (while not physically taxing, you are physically active). Merchandisers will also need to do less paperwork and little evaluation. Mystery shoppers have more of a psychological and mental burden as they have a checklist of responsibilities that require initiation, evaluation, and emotional stability. Mystery shoppers will spend more time filling out forms and reports and writing impressions.

Either way, each has its unique appeals, and they are a great complement from the perspective of potential employers and for you.

Merchandising Paperwork

One appealing factor in merchandising assignments is that there is minimal administrative work. Other than managing your schedule, picking up products, and keeping an occasional audit, you are not going to have to do a lot of paperwork. Being highly efficient at merchandising will allow you to be paid well and still have lots of time for your family and friends. It's a great quality-of-life job!

Merchandising Assignment Availability

You would be surprised how the demand for merchandisers has grown through the years. Retailing is a gigantic multibillion-dollar-a-month industry, and the need for your services as a merchandiser is great! Most shoppers find that they could work virtually any day—and every day—if that is what they want to do.

Know someone who needs a job? Getting into merchandising is a great way to make a fair wage and still enjoy a fun, flexible lifestyle.

The advantages of being a merchandiser far outweigh any disadvantages. I am a retired teacher, and I used to do mystery shopping six or seven days a week, but now I choose merchandising work over the mystery shopping anytime.

Merchandiser Activity Recap

In-Store Merchandising

1. Install POP and Endcap displays
2. Replenish coupons, stickers, and display material
3. Update displays

Store Management

1. Help to communicate excitement and enthusiasm with store personnel
2. Answer questions and fill requests
3. Solve challenges for the store related to your products

Reporting

1. Keep inventory
2. Perform Audits
3. Submit reports on schedule

Store Demos and Vendor Days

1. Perform in-store demos featuring manufacturer products and services
2. Attend trade shows and special events to represent manufacturer

In-Store Training

1. Train store sales staff on features and benefits of manufacturer products and services
2. Provide product-usage training and keep staff up-to-date of upcoming promotions
3. Educate staff on manufacturer's policies and procedures for service, warranties, and refunds

The range of retail establishments that are serviced and maintained by merchandisers is wide and varied:

Department Stores; Grocery Stores; Gas / Convenience Stores; Pet Supply Retailers; Computer Superstores; Bank Branches; Clothing Stores; Toy Stores; Music Stores; Office Supply Stores; Phone Service Retailers; Drug Stores; and many, many more!

CHAPTER 2

Importance of Merchandising

In This Chapter

❖ Good Merchandising Benefits the Customer
❖ Good Merchandising Benefits the Store
❖ Ethical Behavior / Work Quality
❖ Standards of Business Conduct
❖ Client Relations
❖ Merchandisers Who Go the Extra Mile
❖ Service Recovery
❖ Customer Service

Your activities as a merchandiser are vital to a store's ability to sell a manufacturer's products. You will be assuring the proper placement of appealing stand-ups and signs and organizing the shelves. Be sure products are neatly placed. You will set out and replenish brochures and coupons so that customers will pick them up and use them in the purchase of the product. In addition, you will ensure that the right products are out on the sales floor in just the right quantities to have maximum appeal to shoppers.

Furthermore, think of how important it is when you shop that you see only the freshest and more recent product. It is a merchandiser who scours the display area for old or defective stock and to make sure the latest sale pricing is visible.

If you're a more experienced merchandiser who has had a chance to work with a particular manufacturer for a while, then you may even be called upon to provide advice to the store's salespeople or management so that they can better sell the product.

Moreover, if you think these activities mostly benefit the shopper and the store, think again. To the manufacturer, finding a hard worker like you will be like striking gold. That's because you'll become their frontline "face" on their product. You'll be the one who is in touch with what's going on and able to secure enhanced placement for products when it becomes available. And with a little more time, who knows how influential you'll become within your local retail area!

Merchandising is often a first step for good people into an even better career—if they want it. If not, it's one of the best-paying jobs out there that allows you to work at your own pace, on your own schedule, and at the places you choose. It's great flexibility!

Good Merchandising Benefits the Customer

It Makes Shopping Easier

The first aspect of merchandising is how it can be used to attract customers, make shopping easier for them, and give them reasons to come back often and spend more money. Underlying any merchandising plan is the understanding that many consumers no longer consider shopping fun. A retailer's challenge is to use merchandising to take the hassle out of shopping.

It Creates Customer Loyalty

Consumers shop where they feel certain they can find the merchandise they want, and they are generally very loyal customers when stores can create a pleasing shopping experience and provide what they need.

It Promotes Repeat Shopping

Turning shoppers into repeat shoppers is critical. Experts on the subject of store loyalty say that customers who are most likely to come back are those who made a recent purchase, who buy frequently, and who spend the most money. With all the competition for consumer dollars, prime opportunities for growth comes from bringing customers back more often and giving them reasons to buy more each time.

Good Merchandising Benefits the Store

It Enhances a Store's Price Image

Many independent retailers battle a perception among consumers that they are high priced. This is a perception that is heightened by the presence of big-box competition. Merchandisers can play a large role in helping a store develop a value-priced image. With skilled use of product selection, display, and pricing, it can suggest to consumers that they can, indeed, find good prices in independent stores.

It Allows Retailers to Make Strategic Pricing Decisions

Merchandising can also help retailers protect operating margins by increasing item sales at the same time they lower prices. Studies show that by simply moving a product from a shelf location to promotional, sales can double or even triple.

It Increases Sales per Customer

An attractive merchandise arrangement stimulates extra sales and impulse purchases. This boosts sales per customer, which makes a sales record run well above the national average. However, for merchandising to be fully effective, shelves, hooks, bins, feature endcaps, dump bins, and all the other display areas must be full. Stock outs aren't allowed. It takes only one experience of not finding the items they need for do-it-yourselfers to shop elsewhere. Full displays mean accurate inventory tracking and appropriate ordering levels.

Promotes Self-Service Shopping

A retailer can only wait on one customer at a time, but many customers can serve themselves at the same time from the displays built.

It Enhances Sales

Merchandising can suggest related purchases at the point of sale and impulse purchases in a power aisle or at the checkout. Merchandising should complement the efforts of salespeople by organizing the store, suggesting project ideas, reminding customers of forgotten items, promoting special buys and seasonal items, and providing self-shopping information.

It Complements Advertising

Some of the factors that go into improving sales floor productivity include stock turns by department, product line and item, peak-selling periods for each department, and customer traffic patterns.

Merchandising is presenting products in their best light to generate more sales. Whether you are buying at a Target, Kohl's, Dollar Store, a home center, a supermarket, or a toy store, chances are, your buying decision has been influenced by the way the products were merchandised.

Your position as a Merchandiser will be both rewarding and challenging. In your role, you will be expected to help major manufacturing and retail companies present their product to the best advantage in the retail environment. The expertise and experience of good, qualified merchandisers provides the framework for customer satisfaction and the commitment to quality.

Merchandising is not a hobby, but a professional career choice. As in other professions, those who continue to improve their abilities and develop more proficient skills to perform the necessary work will be rewarded with advancement opportunities and increased compensation.

Your client/customer can be any or all of the following:

1. The merchandising company that hired you or asked you to contract with them; the retail store that you are performing the work in.
2. The manufacturer or third party that is paying to have you do the work.
3. The customer in the store who will be buying the product.
4. Your fellow merchandisers who are part of your "team."

While all the "clients" listed above are equally important and each have different expectations of you, they all share the same purpose. That purpose is to provide your clients/customers the most memorable service experience and, in the process, achieve a significant and powerful differentiation from your competitors!

Merchandisers are encouraged to go the extra mile and build strong relationships with valued business partners and understand the client's business and competitors. Nothing ensures loyalty like great service.

To the best merchandisers, clients are important people; you care about them and want to meet and exceed their expectations.

Ethical Behavior / Work Quality

During the course of your employment, you may have access to information of a highly sensitive and confidential nature. Confidential information comes in many forms, including company records, personal information about clients, and business information about products, concepts, processes, services, know-how, client's lists, marketing materials / data, accounting, pricing or salary information, business plans and strategies, negotiations and contracts, and others.

If you encounter confidential information (relating to employees, clients, the corporation, or others), you hold a special position of trust and confidence toward this data.

Standards of Business Conduct

All merchandising companies have established Standards of Conduct. Like all other organizations, merchandising companies require order and discipline to succeed and to promote efficiency, productivity, and cooperation among employees. For this reason, presented below are some examples of conduct that are impermissible and that may lead to corrective action, up to and including immediate discharge. This list is not all-inclusive but does set forth examples of conduct that would be considered impermissible.

- Unauthorized absence from work / no call—no show to work
- Failure to maintain a satisfactory attendance record

- Being convicted or entering a plea of guilty or nolo-contendere to any crime involving theft, breach of fiduciary duty, fraud, or moral turpitude
- Possession, distribution, sale, use of illegal drugs, being under the influence of drugs, alcohol, and/or controlled substances while at work
- Release of confidential information
- Abuse, misuse, or damage to Company property or that of a fellow employee, customer, or visitor
- Violation of posted and/or published safety rules
- Possession of firearms or other types of weapons on Company or customer premises
- Falsification of Company or customer records
- Theft
- Assault or threats of assault or battery
- Abusive language
- Immoral or indecent conduct
- Insubordination
- Smoking in prohibited areas
- Unsatisfactory job performance or conduct

Client Relations

A company's continued success depends on the quality of their relationships with their merchandisers, clients, vendors, and community. The people who serve them form their clients' impression of the company and their willingness to work with them. The merchandisers are the company's ambassadors. The more goodwill they promote, the more the clients will respect and appreciate the company and their services.

Here are some critical requirements that will ensure successful relationships with clients:

- *Always* greet clients in a pleasant, professional, and cheerful manner and with a smile!
- Follow up on all questions and requests promptly and professionally.
- You may not raise your voice to a client or treat clients in a rude, uncooperative, or disrespectful manner.
- You may not engage in an argument with a client. If a client disagrees with you after you have communicated the facts of a situation, simply

listen to the concerns, write them down, and let the client know you will have a manager review the situation and get in touch with them right away.

- When speaking with a client, you may not demean or degrade competitors. Only the facts of a given situation should be stated when necessary.
- You may not talk about specific clients without permission from those clients.

Clients trust merchandisers with their promotional products (coupons, rebates, tools, etc.) and you, as a merchandiser, cannot abuse this trust.

Always remember that your actions reflect on client and store images. Within the stores, and in all your contact with store personnel, you must conduct yourself in an exemplary way. This includes appropriate dress, language, and treatment of people—including team members, customers, and store employees.

1. Always perform the work fully and accurately and report your work in a timely manner.
2. Work your scheduled hours; show up on time, take scheduled breaks, and finish up in the allotted time.

Remember, you have chosen a career in the Service Business. The only product you have is what you can do for your customers.

Merchandisers Who Go the Extra Mile

Merchandisers are encouraged to go the extra mile and build strong relationships with valued business partners and understand the client's business and competitors. Nothing ensures loyalty like these finer points of service:

1. Pay attention to the small details that are important to their customers (internal and external) like accurately completing assigned paperwork and reporting information on time;
2. Are trained to do things that are important, i.e., handling customer problems;

3. Are encouraged to go beyond on customer service.

We merchandisers face a kind of dilemma in our jobs. We are sent to the store by a merchandising company with a certain task to be completed. When we get to the store, the store personnel may instruct us differently. It appears that we work for the merchandising company and the store too.

Our number one job as a merchandiser is to represent, assist, and do service in the store for the merchandising company's client. The store may refuse that assistance. It is their store. They do not have to follow or implement our requests for the client.

From my own experience, here are a few tips to keep in mind when working as a merchandiser:

1. You work for the merchandising company, and they sign your check—not the store manager. Yes, we are to do everything to keep a good working relationship with the store and employees, but we are not to do more than our employer pays us to do. Example: You are instructed to cut in an item, and a department manager wants you to reset a section to accomplish that task. If you have not been authorized to do a reset, you will not be paid for your time.
2. We are "just the messenger." They may refuse the placement of a fixture/display, reset, cut-in, etc.—and that's all right. Don't get in a heated disagreement. It is their store and they can do whatever they want. After bringing the clients' request to the store or department manager's attention and they refuse, then all you can do is to report the existing condition to the client through your paperwork.
3. Speaking of "just being the messenger," I have told more than one department manager not to shoot the messenger. While most store personnel are very helpful and easy to work with, I know that some managers can be difficult. Some are growling when they see a merchandiser approaching. Just keep your chin up and keep smiling. As far as it depends on you, keep a good working relationship by being polite and cooperative. Again, if they refuse your assistance, there is not much you can do. Just report the existing condition.
4. On the other side, some store personnel have a dislike for certain merchandisers because of their actions. (Or they have worked with one

bad merchandiser and think we are all the same.) Some merchandisers show up for resets without first scheduling a time with the department managers. Others wait to do their store visits at the busiest times of day when a department manager must help customers. Others, after a reset, do not clean up their trash and the store personnel are left to clean up after them. Alternatively, they do not follow store rules by taking overstock and returns to the appropriate area as requested (i.e., boxed, labeled, and placed in the right area). Moreover, nothing will frustrate a department manager worse than an uncompleted or improperly completed job. It is then left up to them to go behind and fix a merchandiser's mess.

Before you leave a reset, check in with the department manager to make sure the set meets their approval. Clean up all trash from the reset and place it in the dumpster yourself. Make sure all excess merchandise has been delivered to the appropriate area as instructed. Get to the store as early as possible (even before the store opens to the public) for resets, audits, etc. Again, go the extra mile to have a good working relationship with the store personnel.

Our goal should be to always have a good working relationship with store personnel. A strained relationship will make your job difficult and one you will not enjoy.

Here are a few things you can do to smooth out a difficult relationship with a department manager or store personnel:

1. Sometimes you may request a cut-in per your instructions, and a manager refuses placement. However, you may be able to negotiate an equitable solution, such as placing the product in a different position or as a special display. Place the product to get it out on the sales floor and get it tagged. Nothing will ever sell in the back storage area! Then report the condition to the client through your paperwork.
2. Sometimes a task is "authorized" or "mandatory." In this case, if a department manager refuses, you need to "go over the department manager's head." A talk with the store manager can bring an attitude adjustment. Carefully word your case to the store manager . . . You definitely do not want to be on their bad side!

3. You need to talk to your supervisor. They are almost always very knowledgeable and eager to help you figure these things out. Sometimes a call from your supervisor to the store is all it takes. They can bring a resolution that can suit all parties involved.

If there is anyone out there like me, and I am confident there are thousands of you, I know you take your job seriously and personally—don't lose sleep over this!

You have *not* failed at your job if

1. they refuse assistance/service,
2. you go to a store to place/audit product and it is not even in the store.

Half of a merchandiser's job is just to report conditions so that the client knows what is going on with their product. It is then up to the client to take steps to correct the situation. As long as you have performed this job to the best of your abilities, then that is all you have been asked to do.

Service Recovery

What happens when you don't meet the needs of the client? It is not enough to "just apologize" for failing to meet the client's expectations of your work.

Service recovery is defined as the ability to make things right when foul-ups occur. Service recovery deals with the handling of customer dissatisfaction, customer complaints, and any customer problems, or difficulties with your service. It is when a merchandiser actually turns disappointment into satisfaction—sometimes even into customer delight!

Customer Service

While working in the store as a merchandiser, I am constantly being asked, "Where is the toothpaste?" or whatever else the customer might be searching for. And it is rather amusing how many customers will travel down my aisle . . . must be curiosity. But that is the major reason to get to the store as early as possible or even before the store opens. Less customers = more time to finish our merchandising work without interruptions.

It would be easy to give off the impression that customers are a nuisance, but we should never let that happen. In addition, our demeanor should always be considerate when communicating with the store's customers. When asked where products are located in the store, I try my best to always kindly reply, "I do not work for the store, but let me see if I can help you or find someone who can." The customer should always come first with the store personnel over whatever task we have at hand. Remember, their nuisance is why we have a job!

CHAPTER 3

Types of Merchandising Tasks

In This Chapter

- ❖ Routine Light Merchandising Tasks
- ❖ Performing a Reset
- ❖ Dress for Success
- ❖ Why All the Rules?

There are many different types of merchandising tasks. Not all companies perform all tasks. Some only do resets. Others rarely do resets and mostly perform audits. Some of the more common tasks referred to as light merchandising follows.

Routine Light Merchandising Tasks

Stickering. The action taken to place coupons, rebate stickers, or informational stickers on individual products. It may involve removing any of the above, also.

Placing POP Materials. This involves placing advertising materials (e.g., channel strips, shelf talkers, wobblers, premium pads, etc.). As long as you check in with someone in authority when you get to the store and remember to get your sheet signed and store stamped, if your company requires it, you are home free on this one.

Face out. Ensuring product items are facing out toward the customer. This means, of course, the front of the label is facing out.

Packing-out Product. This is filling a shelf or peg to capacity with product. All you are doing in this assignment is the same work a normal store employee would do. Usually the product is stored in the backroom where you will find it and then load the product on the sales floor.

Auditing. This is an examination and verification of anything from quantity, availability, or pricing. This is one of the easiest tasks you will ever be asked to do. That is, if the store does not throw obstacles in your way. If you are checking the quantity and availability, you will need to get this information from all over the store. That means from the regularly merchandised position, any endcaps, any special displays, and in the stockroom.

Ensuring Shelf (i.e., Modular or Schematic) Integrity. One merchandiser has said, "When I first started working as a merchandiser, I was instructed to 'Ensure the Shelf Integrity.' I thought they wanted me to check if the shelving was sturdy and safe! Ha!" What this really means is to check the shelf or shelves against what you know to be the correct modular, schematic, or planogram and make sure it is set correctly.

Zoning Product. General upkeep of keeping product set to current schematic/planogram. Included in this category would be removing any product that does not belong here. You would make sure each item is on the correct peg, tray, or shelf, e.g., making sure each author's CD is correctly filed behind his name.

Rotating Product. Existing product involves putting new product behind any existing product. Dated items: oldest product is placed in front of newer product so oldest will sell through.

Retagging Product. This involves changing shelf labels on shelf, fixture, or display to update the shelf label information.

Taking Inventory. Taking inventory is an actual physical count of the product in the store. The merchandiser must make sure to get an accurate count in the entire store. If you have store personnel who appreciate the fact that you are doing work that they do not have to do, they will sometimes use what I call their "gun," because it seems to have a different name in every store, to assist you. They can check to see how many of any particular item is supposed to be in the store and then compare your count to it. That way you will know if you need to look for more items to count.

Pulling Product. Removing product is referred to as pulling product. Product may go to returns or be destroyed at store level, depending on your particular instructions.

Cross Merchandising. The action taken to display product along with other related product, i.e., batteries on clip strips placed next to battery-operated toys. This is usually a cut-and-dried activity. In the example, the batteries would come to the store preset on the clip strips with instructions exactly where to place them.

Load and Label. The action taken to load product onto a shelf or peg and to place the corresponding store tag or label for that product.

Pull and Plug. The action taken to pull existing discontinued product and replace with new product. This one is self-explanatory. Just watch out for the usual pitfalls previously mentioned. Remember, always consult with your supervisor if you run into any problems.

Returning Product. Product is returned to vendor or warehouse for reimbursement. The product may be damaged, has an expired date, is no longer carried by the store, or is excess stock. You may be asked to do a credit return for the store too. Just follow their directions.

Cutting-in new product (i.e., Revisions). This is an action taken to place new items on an already-existing display/fixture/shelf by removing old items or reducing the facings of an existing item. Take for example a cosmetic wall. In this case, you would either take off some product that the company is no longer going to be stocking and place the new one in its spot. *On the other hand,* if you have three facings of a couple of colors of nail polish, the company may just cut them down to two facings each and add the new color in the newly created spot. A cut-in usually occurs between major resets.

Building Floor Displays. You build a freestanding display of merchandise that sits on the sales floor. These are typically made of corrugated cardboard. This can be anything from building a PDQ, usually referred to as Pretty Darn Quick, but it really stands for Predetermined Quantity Display. It is rightly named both. It is pretty darn quick to set up if everything goes as planned. That means the product is there; it is located somewhere in the stockroom that it can be got out, and the location it is assigned for it to be placed is cleared. It is stocked as a Predetermined Quantity Display if nothing on it was damaged beyond selling during shipping.

Performing a Reset

Another merchandising task is performing resets. Resets are the updating and changing of shelving/fixtures/products to conform to authorized or preferred configuration

Resets are *not* considered Light Merchandising. There are small resets that take only a few hours to complete and do not involve a lot of weight lifting or bending. One person typically completes these resets. Other resets may last a day or longer and involve repeated bending and lifting. These types of resets may be done as a team with other merchandisers. Resets will be covered in detail in a later chapter.

Typical Light Merchandising Store Visit

Let us take a look at what you would do working as a merchandiser on a typical light merchandising store visit.

The day before the job, you would review and organize all your projects. Plan what must be done the following day. Now would be the time to call the supervisor with any questions.

On the day of the visit

1. Get to store as early as possible. You will have more time to communicate to the department managers and there will be fewer customers.
2. Put on your company-supplied name tag identifying yourself as a merchandiser (or the store supplied generic name tag).

3. Sign in on the Vendors' Log. To identify vendors and visitors in their stores, retailers use a Vendors' Log. It is usually located at the customer service counter or in the receiving department.
4. Find a shopping cart to use as a portable workspace. Every now and then, you will run into a store that will not let you use a shopping cart. Their reason being they only have a few and they must be left for the customers.
5. Check in with the department manager or the person in charge to let them know what you plan to accomplish that day and ask any questions you may have. It is best to ask everything you could possibly need at this one time. They will not take kindly to repeat interruptions. If the department manager can't answer your questions, then you will need to call your supervisor if available or have them return a call to the store. Most supervisors understand there will be questions and prefer that merchandisers ask if they are in doubt.
6. Proceed to the department you will be working in today.
7. Compare the area to your planogram and instructions. Now is the time to note any questions, both for your store contact and possibly for your supervisor.
8. While you are in the store, you will make sure the client's products are set according to planogram (the diagram showing the exact authorized location of each product) and that the correct tag is displayed for the correct products.
9. Stock the client's products on the shelves and clip strips and dust the display and product.

If the client's products are getting low or out of stock, you will request the store to place an order. Sometimes, ordering is the responsibility of the merchandiser and you will follow the instructions provided by your company to place an order. Do not be surprised if you are told that their system automatically places orders when a certain level is reached in their inventory system. You should also not be surprised if you are told, "Oh, we have that product in the back. It will be stocked by the night shift." When you offer to stock it, you are often turned down for one reason or another. See, you must learn early that there are many department managers out there that are territorial.

If you find that some of the client's product is missing a label, then you would request or print labels for those products. If the client has supplied promotional displays or signage, then you will place or set up these items. You may also be instructed to cut in new product or return recalled, damaged, or date-expired product.

If the merchandising company has supplied a Job Review Questionnaire (JRQ) to be filled out, you will accurately complete it while you are still in the store. After all objectives are completed, it is a good idea to go over the report form with the department manager when asking for their signature on it. This is also your opportunity to tell them what you have completed that day and state any unresolved problems that may have been encountered. After the Department Manager signs your paperwork, you may need to get a store stamp if required by the merchandising company. (The stamp is usually located in the claims department or store manager's office.) After the paperwork is completed, sign out of vendor's log by noting the time you are leaving.

On the same daythat you complete your projects, you will report to the merchandising company as required. If you are responsible for placing orders to individual companies that supply the store, you will call in/ fax orders for stocks that are fresh out or low in supply. You finish by double-checking your paperwork and then mailing or faxing along with time sheets if required. Each company handles their paperwork differently. Just make sure you follow their directions accurately and completely.

Any special or exceptional circumstances are reported in the comments area, e.g.the product was extremely dirty, there was outdated product on the shelf, the product was in disarray and not attractively presented on the shelf, etc.

Dress for Success

While on the job as a merchandiser, your appearance is a declaration of who you are. When you take the time to dress for success, you tell store personnel and customers you come in contact with that you are inspired and proficient.

These same tips apply to dressing for a job interview. Many of us object to being evaluated for employment based on how we look. We prefer to be hired because of our competence and qualifications, not because of our attire and grooming. But like it or not, appearance is important too.

Personal grooming is just as important as what you wear. You may select the right clothes, but neglecting personal hygiene can ruin the image you wish to present. What is ordinary every day to most of us is sometimes a chore for others, so I will throw out what is expected: neatly trimmed or manicured nails; teeth brushed and fresh breath—beware of foods, tobacco, coffee, and alcohol, which may leave breath odor. Freshly bathed/showered, always use deodorant. Men—freshly shaved, mustache or beard neatly trimmed. Women—use makeup sparingly and be natural looking.

Your company's standing is maintained by the appearance its merchandisers present to the clients, customers, and team members. Therefore, it is extremely important that you dress in a professional manner at all times. Know your company's policy on dress code and grooming.

As a professional merchandiser, it is important to

- maintain a neat and clean appearance;
- use good judgment in selecting on-the-job clothing;
- for safety reasons, bare upper arms and legs, open-toed shoes, or flip-flop sandals are not allowed;
- cutoff or ripped jeans, T-shirts with off-color or offensive wording, halter, or tank tops and swimwear are considered inappropriate at any work site;
- torn, tattered, or dirty clothing is never acceptable;
- revealing clothing is unacceptable;
- proper undergarments must be worn at all times;
- a neat, professional hairstyle—a short, simple hairstyle is better, but long hair is acceptable if it is clean and styled so that it is not in your face;
- wear your name tag at all times;
- don't wear strong-smelling perfumes or aftershave/cologne. Your scent should not linger after you leave.

Merchandisers will need to check with their respective merchandising companies on policies that refer to

- hats, sunglasses, and jewelry;

- body piercing and nose rings;
- clothing items for a specific client; such as vests, name tags, etc.

When doing resets, the clothing is somewhatcasual. At this time sometimes, at the client's discretion, you can wear clean jeans with no rips or tears and tops of a more relaxed fit, still keeping in mind the following list of no-nos. There are still some clothing that is not optional at any time, in any form, or for any reason: sports jerseys; tops that expose the midriff; bulky hooded sweatshirts; scrubs; tops that don't cover the back when bending; denim; jogging suits; spandex; leggings; miniskirts; shorts; ratty jeans; pants with hems dragging; pants with permanent dirt marks; dirty, ugly, old tennis shoes; hats.

Here are a few other rules a company I currently work for enforces:

Hair must be pulled back; no unapproved head gear; one necklace (long necklaces prohibited); shirt must remain tucked; pants worn at the waist; one bracelet or watch per hand; no visible piercings other than one set of post style earrings (remove or cover piercings); tattoos must be covered by clothing or other covering.

Check the mirror and see what others see. If it's too tight or too loose, don't wear it! When in doubt, dress with the most conservative option available.

Many of us seem to wear polo shirts and often get mistaken for store employees. Most store employees now wear polos, khaki or cargo pants, and aprons. So I thought this would be a good place for a little helpful info for merchandisers to know what colors to avoid at what stores. *But then*, everybody started changing their colors and messed up my plan.

To summarize the dress code section, a company's dress code is very important to their company and their customers. Make sure that you strictly adhere to the dress code. A professional appearance is critical to the company's success.

Why All the Rules?

1. Safety is the most important reason for the dress code. Long necklaces, earrings, inappropriate clothing, etc., can cause serious safety risks.
2. The company dress code unites their team. All team members can easily be identified to help each other.
3. The company's reputation is built on their delivery of service, their integrity, and their professional appearance. A professional appearance reinforces your reputation with your customers.

CHAPTER 4

The Tools and Knowledge of Merchandising

In This Chapter

❖ Merchandising Tools
❖ Reset Tools
❖ Label Info—Line by Line
❖ Working In the Store

Merchandising Tools

There are certain tools that you will find necessary to complete various tasks as a merchandiser. You may not need all these tools when you first begin, but in time you will find that you need most of them. Some companies supply tools or reimburse you for the expense. If not, for a few dollars, you can stock your own merchandisers' bag with the essentials.

Reset Tools

- *Name tag*—Wear your name tag always while in the store
- *Soft-sided Briefcase*—Get a legal-sized one to keep all your forms organized neatly.

The following items should go in your briefcase:

- *Feather Duster*—A feather duster has always been known as the merchandiser's best friend, but lately, I am finding that some of the microfiber dusters work better in many cases. Instead of just spreading the dust around, they attract it and carry it away.

- *Clipboard*—The legal size is better because many of your forms are of legal size now. Also, if possible, get a metal one, or you will find yourself replacing it often.
- *Ink Pen*—Use this to fill out forms and your report and mileage forms in the store.
- *Wite Out*—Always have this on hand for little mistakes on report forms.
- *Calculator*—For those times you need to write a credit.
- *Three-ring Binder*—To hold forms, instructions, your company's information, and your supervisor's telephone number.
- *Fine-tip Felt Pen*—This type of pen will work on all labels if you need to handwrite them.
- *Large Felt Pen Marker*—This is handy for labeling boxes.
- *Scissors*—Always handy to have.
- *Wet Ones*—You would not believe how dirty you can get on a reset.

The following items should fit in a small tool bag. Wal-Mart, and perhaps other chains, sells a small tool bag in pink, brown, or black that has most of the following and much, much more at a very reasonable price.

- *Hammer*—On resets where shelves must be moved, it gives new life to old shelving that refuses to adjust to its new home.
- *Rubber Mallet*—This is handy to keep from denting stubborn, stuck shelves.
- *Tape Measure*—To measure shelving heights and lengths.
- *Pliers*—Straighten out bent fixtures, shelving, and whatever else.
- *Screwdrivers*—Flat-head and Phillips.
- *Box Cutter*—To open and break down boxes.
- *Flat-edge Razor*—One that holds the blade flat to scrape.
- *Label Peeler*—If your company doesn't supply one, try a plastic grapefruit peeler. Label peelers help lift existing labels off the shelf and make it easier on your fingers and nails. A citrus peeler is good to use for this.
- *Ruler or Yardstick cut to eighteen inches*—To easily straighten product on the shelf or to push over small items in the set.
- *Goo Gone*—To get the sticky residue off the molding left by tags.

The following items you should be able to get at the store level.

- *Step Stool*
- *Cleaning Supplies*
- *Garbage Bag*

The following items you will need to have at home:

- *Computer with Internet Connection*—More and more job offers and reporting are done via the Internet.
- *File Cabinet*—To save your completed projects and time/expense forms.
- *Excel Viewer*—Most new computers now come with Microsoft Excel. The Microsoft Excel 97 Viewer allows users to view and print Excel 97 and Excel 2000 spreadsheet files, in addition to other Excel for Windows (versions 2.0 and greater) and Excel for the Macintosh (versions 2.2a and greater) spreadsheet files. This freely distributable small viewer gives users the flexibility to view page layout, copy ad control cell sizes, and access the zoom and AutoFilter features.
- *Word Viewer*—As with Excel, most new computers now come equipped with Microsoft Word. With the Microsoft Word Viewer 97/2000, Microsoft Word users can share documents with those who do not have Word, and users without Word can open and view Word documents. This product also allows users who wish to post rich-text-formatted Word documents on the Internet to expand their online audience to people who might not have Word. This viewer also allows users to view and print documents created in the Word native file format, even if they do not have Word. Users are allowed to zoom, outline, or view page layout, headers/footers, footnotes, and annotations.
- Business Forms—I have included several of these in the Resource number 3—Business Forms.

Label Info—Line by Line

Shelf labels (a.k.a. Shelf Tags) contain valuable information that is essential to a merchandiser. They identify what product is authorized to be in that space on the shelf or fixture and include the product description, count/size and price. Shelf labels typically contain a Universal Product Code (UPC) symbol and store's individual stock number.

Let's get up close and personal with a UPC Symbol, one of the components of the shelf label. The twelve-digit UPC symbol is used by almost every manufacturer on their product packaging.

UPCs are used by different people for many different reasons. Some examples are the following:

UPCs can be used by the store and product manufacturers to measure a product's movement or sales. By scanning the UPC code at the check out, consumers can review the Cash Registers' receipt showing price and product description. Merchandisers and store employees use the UPC symbol for ordering (and checking for product that is already ordered and in transit), monitoring on-hand inventories, identification of products and cases, creating shelf labels, and more. The UPC symbol on product packaging has two parts: the machine-readable bar code and the human-readable twelve-digit UPC number.

The **bar code** is a scannable line graphic and is assigned to that product by the manufacturer. It is a code pattern of bar stripes of different widths, which can be read by electronic scanner.

Under the Bar Code on the packaging, UPC symbol is the **UPC number**. These numbers, usually twelve digits long, are assigned by the Uniform Code Council. The Uniform Code Council developed this system in the early 1970s.

The UPC number on product packaging is made up of four components:

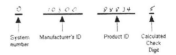

The System number is the first number that appears to the left of the bar code. The following table shows the category that each system number represents.

0	Standard UPC number (regular grocery products or prepackaged standard weight items.)
1	Reserved
2	Random-weight items (fruits, vegetables, meats, etc.)
3	Health and Beauty Aids (HBA) items (over-the-counter medications, shampoo, etc)
4	In-store marking for retailers (A store can set up its own codes, but no other store will understand them.)
5	Coupons
6	Standard UPC number for Private Label Manufacturer's
7	Standard UPC number (same items as System number 0)
8	Reserved
9	Reserved

Manufacturer's ID: The manufacturer identification number is the next five digits of the UPC number. This is a unique number assigned by the UPC Council to that manufacturer only.

Product ID: The next five digits are the product identification number. This is a number assigned by the manufacturer to identify products in the same category such as Little Kitty Liver flavor versus the Chicken flavor or different size boxes of Krispy puffed rice.

Calculated Check Digit or Module Check Character is the last digit of the UPC code and is on the far right in the bar code. This number is the result of a mathematical calculation using the first eleven numbers in the UPC number. The check digit ensures the UPC number was composed, keypunched, or scanned correctly.

UPCs may also appear as **Suppressed codes** that reduce the twelve-digit number to less numbers by removing zeros. It is used to mark small items, and it is only available to companies whose Manufacturer's ID number starts with a zero (0). These suppressed codes are often used on difficult to scan small or round products such as cosmetics, soda, and candy items.

The **European Article Number** or EAN is the European equivalent of the UPC. The code differs from its American counterpart by including a two-digit system number that represents the country in which the product is manufactured. Its unique identification numbers are regulated by the International Article Numbering Association. These thirteen-digit codes identify country, manufacturer, item number, and check digit. I have never had to work with EAN, but you want to be aware of them. If you were to encounter one, it would probably be found on candy or holiday cookies.

Now, let's look more closely at the shelf label. Not all store labels contain all of the following. Some only list one feature and no others.

Let's look at the below examples of a shelf label and product packaging UPC. Look on the shelf label UPC number (arrow pointing to it on the below example). Notice that the system number and the check digit on the package's UPC number are omitted on this store chains shelf label.

The **Stock Number** (i.e., ordering or store item number) is usually listed. It is an additional number issued to each item in a store by a particular chain. This number is used for reordering from the warehouse. These numbers change from chain to chain. (In Wal-Mart, they assign a seven-digit

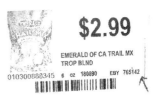

number that is located under the bar code on the shelf label. The first two digits always represent the department number.) Some stores just use the UPC number as their stock number.

Labels may contain the **date** the label was printed. This is helpful if you are sent to the store to verify a section of products has been recently updated by a reset

Labels may show how the product is ordered. For instance, on a Wal-Mart label, if there is a small WR in the left-hand corner, this means the product is stocked in the Wal-Mart Distribution Center and, when ordered, will be delivered in two to five days. If in the bottom left corner there is an AD, this means the product is mass-ordered by Wal-Mart from the manufacturer's warehouse and then distributed to the individual stores. This is called an assembly product and takes up to one and one half weeks to be delivered.

Each store has different terminology for the labels' info. Just to confuse you more, there is one more term you should be aware of. **SKU** stands for Stock-Keeping Unit and is a number associated with a product for inventory purposes. This number is used to identify an individual product by specific size, shape, color, flavor, or style. Some stores refer to the UPC number as the SKU. Others refer to the stores' particular stock number as the SKU. Check with your particular store or supervisor to clarify.

Labels are usually placed on the outermost edge of the shelf on the shelf molding. The label is affixed just below the product and is on the left-hand side of the first facing. A facing is the number of shelf spaces a store has authorized for the product to occupy.

The reason for placing to the left of the first facing is when the stock person comes to stock products they know that the label is the starting point for each product. Some stores center their labels in the middle of the product. Look at your store to see how they position their labels.

Each store affixes their labels differently. Some peel off only half of the sticky backing and then place. Others peel off all the sticky backing and place. If unsure, check for other labels in the store to see how they are affixed.

Using a handheld scanner, you can scan bar codes and print shelf labels at your store. Other names for the handheld scanner include Telxon, 960 unit, LRT, RMU, and more, depending on which store chain you at working for. Handhelds can be used with a portable printer (a.k.a. Label Maker) or some may send the data to the backroom where you can pick up your labels. The unit will also scan the tag or bar code on a product and then you can order, audit, survey, get an inventory count, etc.

You can manually type in the UPC number or stock code for your chain and print a label too. Sometimes it is necessary to include the system or check digit when manually typing in a UPC. Others times you don't need one or both. Sometimes your paperwork will show a UPC number and will / will not show the check digit. I have no explanation for this, except you should be aware of the fact. You can also print labels by scanning the UPC symbol on a product packaging.

A few stores do not have handheld scanners, and all their labels come from the corporate headquarters. If you have missing/damaged tags, and the store cannot supply printed labels, you will have to handwrite labels. Get blank tags from the department manager. Most stores require the following info on the tag: description, UPC number, their item or stocking code number, and price. You can then place the tag in the appropriate space.

A **Tag Run** (i.e., Row run) is a printout of all labels needed for a specific category in the store. Tag runs will be further explained in a later chapter.

An **EAS Label or Tag** is a special tag attached and/or adhered to product, which will alarm when passed through an EAS detection equipment. You may be asked to verify if products have EAS labels on them. It is easily identifiable. It is placed on the product near the bar code on the package and is thicker than paper with a metallic appearance.

Even though I have only seen **Electronic Tags** in my stores used on tobacco products, they may be used more abundantly in your area. It is a digital display unit attached through electrical connections to the price molding of the shelf, which displays the price of an item. Special keys are used to change the digital information.

Working in the Store

Introduce yourself to the sales floor team leaders who work in your merchandise area. This person will be your contact for questions on the sales floor regarding zoning, flexing, and making signs and labels.

Daily Routine

Follow these steps on the sales floor:

- Find the sales floor areas where the vendor merchandise needs to be stocked.
- Zone the area completely. (Look for missing signs and labels, face out product on shelves; ensure product is aligned with the right shelf labels.)
- Scan the items on the sales floor that need to be stocked.
- When scanning, write down the item and backroom location of each item scanned.

Here is an example of how to read a shelf label.

1. Description
2. Retail price
3. DPCI—Target Code Number
4. Schematic number—this tells you the planogram section the shelf number and the exact product location on that shelf or peg
5. Number of facings
6. Date label was printed
7. Last digits of the UPC code
8. UPC bar code

Follow these steps in the stockroom:

- Go to the backroom and find the locations of this Merchandise.
- Pull the merchandise to be filled. **Important! If you pull the last of the item from a specific location, make sure you follow the proper**

procedure for that store to notify them that there aren't any more of the item in the location.

- Stock the merchandise to the sales floor.
- Confirm that all authorized displays are up and stocked.
- Take care of any garbage and cardboard by using the compactor and cardboard bailer.
- Generate any missing ESV/Sale signs or missing labels.
- Do not hesitate to ask questions from the sales floor team leaders or Backroom Captain.

The Stockroom

Stockrooms can differ in many ways. Some stores have only one stockroom. Some have multilevel stockrooms. Others have one main stockroom, plus some smaller stockrooms that contain product for specific departments (e.g., electronics). Stores may even have containers, trailers, or off-site locations with merchandise in them.

Note: Risers are an extension of the stockroom; merchandise on risers must be removed from its location with a handheld unit to update the Stockroom Location System.

Stockroom Labels

Stockroom labels identify the location of merchandise in the stockroom. Finding merchandise in the stockroom is as easy as understanding the labels.

1. Each stockroom is broken down by aisle, and each aisle is numbered.
2. Each aisle is divided into sections.
3. Each section is assigned a letter that identifies it.
4. Each shelf in the section has a numerical identification that assigns it to a specific stockroom location.

CHAPTER 5

The Elements of Merchandising

In This Chapter

❖ Sales Floor Layouts
❖ Use of Interior Signage
❖ Use of Space
❖ Use of Color
❖ Use of Lighting

There's more to merchandising than you might realize. Merchandising is much more than attractive displays. It incorporates sales floor design, product selection, product presentation, pricing, and interior signing. Merchandising is the effective use of products, display fixtures, space, color, lighting, and signing to encourage customers to buy.

Most stores are departmentalized, and customers are accustomed to shopping this way. They like organized stores, and most like to be able to find merchandise quickly and easily on their own, even if they need help from a store sales associate. All the elements of merchandising, when working together, will help accomplish this.

Sales Floor Layouts

Grid Layout. This is the simple, traditional layout for stores, with straight cross aisles leading off one or more main aisles into departments. This layout is neat and makes good use of space. Its main drawback is that it does not put the maximum amount of product in front of customers.

Loop / Racetrack Layout. This layout has the main traffic aisle circling the sales floor. It gives every major department exposure on the main aisle. It moves customers through the store and lets them see merchandise in more departments. It provides more locations for endcaps, which helps create a value price image.

Diagonal Layout. This is a modification of the loop / racetrack layout and can be effective in smaller stores. It creates several triangular areas in the store and pulls customers to corners they might otherwise miss.

Power Aisle. This design works well for smaller sales floors where a loop or racetrack is not practical. It is a double-width aisle that runs the full length of the store.

Departmental Cross Aisles. These aisles feed off the power aisle. The power aisle gives exposure to most major departments through the use of feature endcaps and provides room for impulse or promotional mass displays in the center of the aisle. It makes maximum use of display area.

Project Centers and Demonstration Areas. These areas can be developed with any sales floor layout. They can be used for classes, workshops, or product demonstrations as well as collection points for how-to videos, books, and other kinds of take-home project and product information. These areas should present products related to projects and focus attention on promoted merchandise. Signing should suggest projects, explain product features, benefits, and price, and highlight the value of home improvement projects. For people want to participate in shopping and classes, clinics and demonstrations appeal to this desire.

Cube Display. This is another way smaller stores can get the maximum amount of merchandise on the sales floor. It means using higher fixtures with careful attention to the kinds of merchandise displayed on higher shelves. An effective way to use cube display is to put the higher fixtures in the back of the store to make more merchandise visible from the front and lead customers through the store.

Use of Interior Signage

Makes Shopping Easier. Signage is key to making shopping easier for customers and giving them information to make intelligent buying decisions. Signs keep customers in the store longer, move them from department to department, and suggest more items to purchase. In addition to department and aisle signs, shelf and product signs can convey shopping information.

Provides Information. Signs should tell price, savings, features, benefits, and uses of products. They can create urgency by identifying items as one-time-only bargains or closeouts. They should be neat, easily read, eye-catching, and informative. Informational signs should describe the product, state its price, identify advertised items, flag new items, etc. In addition to giving customers instantaneous information, item/price signs help establish a value-price image.

Department Signs. These signs should be visible from the front of the store to help time-pressed customers quickly find what they are looking for. Departmental signs are different from decor and point-of-sale signs. They should be a regular part of your merchandise arrangement. They help any store, but they are essential on any sales floor that is five thousand square feet or larger.

How-to Project Signs. These signs provide information at the point of sale that will tell customers about the product and suggest project ideas. How-to signage can be especially effective with related item or cross merchandising.

Point-of-Purchase Signs. Good point-of-purchase (POP) signs can stimulate additional sales. An effective point-of-purchase sign will:

• Attract the shopper's attention
• Identify the item or service offered
• Describe what the item will do for the shopper
• Give the price and any savings

Use of Space

Making Productive Use of Space. Merchandising should organize products to make the most productive use of space. This involves setting shelves at heights that will clear merchandise but not waste space, adjusting hooks and bins to the size of the item, and fitting long—and short-handled items together.

Determining Which Products to Put Where. Retailers advertise products they think customers want. That same idea should govern what items are put in prime display space in the store. Keep the best display area for high-demand, fast-moving products. Putting slow-movers in prime space won't make them sell faster; it will only suggest to customers that the merchandise they want is in another store.

Use of Color

Attracting with Color. Color attracts customer attention, whether the color is in the packaging or in the product itself. Take advantage of color in organizing displays. Surrounding color—walls, fixtures, etc.—should complement the merchandise; it should not distract customer attention away from products and packages.

Use of Lighting

Setting the Mood. Lighting does more than let customers find their way through the store. It sets a mood and creates a shopping environment. Bright, well-lighted stores are more appealing than dark, poorly lighted ones.

Drawing Attention. Lighting can draw attention to feature departments and highlight special areas of the store. It can enhance the color and appearance of merchandise. For maximum effect, lighting should be replaced on a regular basis and before bulbs burn out. Fixtures should be cleaned every time lighting is changed.

CHAPTER 6

Types of Fixtures and Displays

- ❖ Types of Fixtures
- ❖ Shelf Accessories
- ❖ Types of Point of Purchase (POP)
- ❖ Types of Displays

Types of Fixtures

Ninety percent of all planograms are set on the gondolas varying in sizes from two feet to over forty feet. There are other types of fixtures that will also use planograms to show the placement of product. Some other types are 4-ways, Spinners, Greeting Card Fixtures, Promo tables, Endcaps, Cosmetic Fixtures, and finally, Walls. The basics we are going to talk about can be used with all fixtures, and it will enable you to set most any planogram.

By definition, a fixture is any shelf, display, or case that is made to hold product. Let us start by looking at the individual shelving units that make up the gondolas that in turn make the aisles.

A **shelving unit** is the physical permanent fixture used with pegs or shelves to display a product. It is also the general term used in describing gondolas, side counters, in-line fixtures, and modulars.

Shelving units are divided into **sections**, usually three or four feet wide, which are combined to create an aisle.

The main bottom section of the shelving unit, next to the floor, is the **base**. The bottom shelf sits on top of this and never changes its position.

Next comes the **back wall** of the shelving unit. This can be made of pegboard, gridwall, slatwall, or uniweb.

The **upright bars** attached to the back wall of the shelving unit and hold the shelves in place. **Shelves** are usually attached to these bars in one of two ways. They can have brackets already attached to them. On the

other hand, **shelf brackets**, similar to metal arms, are attached to the bars and the shelves are placed on top of them.

Channel moldings are the front edge of the shelf where shelf tags, labels, and advertising messages are placed.

Fencing is usually made of short wire that looks like a fence in your yard. It can be used to separate smaller items on the same shelf. Alternatively, it can be used on the front edge of the shelf to hold and prevent small objects from falling off slanted shelves.

The **riser** is the top shelf over the shelving unit and is used to store overstocks. These overstocks must relate to the product directly beneath it and should be tagged. The space below the riser, but above the top shelf, is called the

cheater shelf and has no products assigned to it. The department manager can usually use this space at their discretion.

Now that we have built the fixture, we need to decide what types of shelf accessories are available to make this work with the type of product we are merchandising.

Shelf Accessories Include the Following:

Peg Hooks. Metal or plastic hooks that are used to merchandise small hanging product. These are used for candy, general merchandise, and health and beauty care.

Overlays. Pieces of plastic on the end of peg hooks that hold the shelf tag/label.

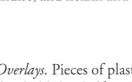

Snap Railing. A rail with pegs attached that slide.

J-Hook. A hook that extends out from the shelf to hang merchandise on.

Sidekick (Powerwing). A product display that is typically metal and hangs on the side of endcap shelving.

Clip Strip. Type of display that can be metal or plastic and hangs vertically by a hook from the shelf. Merchandise clipped on this strip is usually impulse items. The strips are displayed throughout the store.

Types of Point of Purchase (POP)

Point of Purchase (POP). This can refer to a display unit, such as a floor display or sidekick preloaded with product from the manufacturer, placed in the store. Or it can be advertising materials placed, stuck, or hung near the product it is advertising. When placed at or near the cash register area, they are called Point-of-Sale (POS) Materials or display.

Counter Card. A display card used at the checkout or at a service counter. Counter cards may be with merchandise or to serve as a sales promotion or reminder.

Brochure Holders. This may be POS or POP.

Instant Redeemable Coupons (IRCs). These are usually placed directly on the product.

Neck Hanger Tag. This is placed on peg or product such as bottleneck.

Pole Topper. An upright fixture used in a merchandise display to hold POP or POS signing materials.

Channel Strips (Shelf Strips). An advertising message for shelf stock, affixed to the channel molding.

Shelf Talker (Bean Flip, Shelf Tag). A small sign that sticks or attaches to the channel (shelf) molding draw customers' attention to the product and stimulate sales at the point of purchase. It usually gives some details of the product or promotional information.

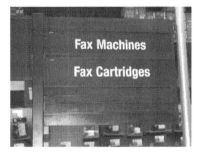

Table Tent. A cardboard or plastic sign folded like a tent that sits on a tabletop or counter to advertise an item

Header Cards. Signage placed in a permanent header fixture that can be removed and replaced.

Tear-off pads. These are sheets of paper that can be removed one at a time by the consumer. They give information about the product that they are placed near.

Stickers. These include coupons, rebate offers, product updates, or corrections of information on the packaging.

Types of Displays

There are various types of displays that you use every day in your merchandising efforts. Each one plays a unique role in a store's overall merchandising efforts, and each has the ability to dramatically increase sales of the products merchandised in them.

All the different types of displays in a store work in conjunction with one another to provide a better and more organized shopping environment for customers. They can help stimulate impulse purchases and give a store a better price image. Customers will get bored if they see the same displays twice and stop considering shopping in your store.

The goal of any display is to grab attention. Promotional displays are generally at the entrance of the store, or in a high-traffic area, like a walkway. Signage is a great way to communicate to your customers as well. Lighting, fully stocked garment racks, and helpful employees are also necessary.

Retail stores can benefit greatly from utilizing retail gridwall and retail slatwall fixtures. These commercial strength displays do something that regular clothing racks cannot. They get all your merchandise right up in the customer's line of sight. They also clear out floor space, making the store easy to navigate for customers, reducing the places for shoplifters to hide, and making room for any extra holiday or promotional items that you may have coming in.

Slatwall and gridwall both have detachable hooks, bars, clamps, and shelves that can easily be moved and rearranged to give you the most pleasing display possible. Employees or merchandisers can simply move the fixtures left or right, up or down to get the spacing right between merchandise. On a gridwall or a slatwall, you can easily combine like items on to one peg, bar, or shelf.

Endcap

What It Is

The displays at the end of each gondola run are called feature ends or *endcaps* and are highly effective. Whether or not endcaps are signed for special pricing, consumers assume the items stocked on them are on sale. Some manufacturers create displays with endcaps in mind, while many wholesalers have special programs that offer endcap displays and a seasonal rotation schedule.

Why Endcaps Work

1. Consumers expect to see endcaps in a retail store.
2. They expect to see sharp prices on the merchandise displayed there.
3. They highlight fashion items such as housewares and decorating products.
4. They help close out overstocked inventory.
5. They draw customers off the power aisle and into departments.
6. They help you develop a competitive price image.
7. They appeal to customers' desire to save time and money.

The Effectiveness of Endcaps Depends on the Following

1. The display's attractiveness
2. Location in the store
3. Relationship to surrounding merchandise
4. Price
5. How well it has been advertised or promoted
6. Ease of accessibility

How to Use for Best Results

1. Promote price specials and special buys.
2. Choose low-priced consumables.
3. Promote new items and call attention to seasonal items.
4. Tie in with advertised specials.
5. Mass display items to clear out overstocks.
6. Display related items. Limit the number of different items to two or three. Choose related items.
7. Design displays to increase customer convenience.
8. Design signing to inform customers.
9. Change frequently on a rotating schedule.

Permanent Dump Bin

What It Is

Permanent dump bins are power aisle displays that should be used to merchandise one-time special buys or closeouts. They are generally made of wire, so the color in the product packaging can help attract additional attention.

Why Permanent Dump Bins Work

1. They create a sense of urgency to buy at a value price.
2. They promote a closeout-type sale.
3. They promote a special deal the store is passing on to customers.
4. They focus on products that customers can use every day.
5. They project the image of a special price that will not last long.
6. They contribute to a competitive price image.
7. They appeal to consumers' desire to save time and money.

How to Use for Best Results

1. Choose products that have broad appeal.
2. Choose items that customers use every day.
3. Choose consumable products.
4. Choose low-ticket items.
5. Choose items that can be sold for a very good price.
6. Choose items that can be easily picked up.
7. Promote special one-time buys.
8. Use colorful items to attract attention.
9. Fill the dump bin with a single product and keep it full.
10. Use signs to suggest a special sale or blowout price.
11. Change the product selection frequently.
12. Tie in with advertised specials.

Temporary Dump Bin

What It Is

Like permanent dump bins, temporary dump bins are power aisle displays that should be used to merchandise one-time special buys or closeouts. The difference is that their disposable nature suggests a limited time offer, which appeals to bargain hunters. They are generally made of cardboard and are supplied by manufacturers.

Why Temporary/Disposable Dump Bins Work

1. They produce significant sales increases.

2. They create a sense of urgency.
3. They focus on seasonal products—needed now!
4. They project the image of a special price that will not last long.
5. They appeal to consumers' desire to save money and time.
6. They contribute to a competitive price image.
7. They promote extra bargains in the power aisle.
8. They make shopping more enjoyable and fun.

How to Use for Best Results

1. Choose seasonal products.
2. Choose low-ticket items.
3. Choose items that can be easily picked up.
4. Limit product selection to two or three items.
5. Keep the display full and neat.
6. Use signs to suggest a special sale.
7. Change the product selection frequently.
8. If the dump bin becomes damaged or worn, replace it.

Checkout Display

What It Is

Checkout displays are impulse-driven displays that remind customers of something they might have forgotten. Either they can be contained in a cardboard merchandiser, placed in wire racks or peg hooks next to the checkout counter, or placed directly on the sales counter.

Why Checkout Displays Work

1. Everyone who comes into the store passes the checkout on the way out.
2. Checkout counter displays remind customers of something they may have forgotten.
3. They promote impulse sales.
4. They put products within easy reach.
5. They create a sense of urgency.

6. They turn an unattractive backside of a checkout counter into prime-selling area.
7. They appeal to consumers' urge to save money.
8. They add excitement to shopping.

How to Use for Best Results

1. Choose items that excite consumer interest.
2. Choose impulse items.
3. Choose consumable items.
4. Choose items most customers recognize and use.
5. Choose low-priced items.
6. Choose items that will not be damaged by handling.
7. Keep merchandise off the checkout counter; use the display area at the front of the checkstand.

Service Counter Display

What It Is

Like checkout displays, service counter displays are impulse-driven displays that remind customers of something they might have forgotten. Since customers often spend time waiting at the service counter for a service to be performed, these displays usually consist of a plastic or cardboard merchandisers or items placed directly on the service counter.

Why Service Counter Displays Work

1. Displays suggest an additional purchase.
2. They remind customers of something they may have forgotten.
3. They give customers something to look at and think about while they wait.
4. They may suggest another project.
5. They may generate conversation that can lead to another sale or future project.
6. They put products within easy reach.
7. They can turn empty counter space into productive selling area.
8. They appeal to customers' desire to save money and time.
9. They add interest to shopping.

10. They create a sense of urgency.

How to Use for Best Results

1. Choose items that are small.
2. Choose items that are not likely to be knocked off or spilled.
3. Choose items that will not be damaged by handling.
4. Choose impulse items.
5. Choose consumable items.
6. Choose items most customers recognize and use.
7. Choose items that relate to the type of service being offered.
8. Position items carefully—where consumers will see them but where they will not be in the way.
9. Consider items that need a little explanation to generate questions that would result in sales.

Rolling Rack

What It Is

As the name suggests, rolling racks are display units on wheels, usually consisting of a steel frame with several shelves made of wire. They are easily moved from place to place on the sales floor to make productive use of limited space.

Why Rolling Racks Work

1. Rolling racks highlight related products in high-visibility areas.
2. They make productive use of small space.
3. They are adaptable; they can be used anywhere in the store, even outside.
4. They display several different products but require minimum inventory.
5. They can be moved easily and frequently.
6. They create a sense of urgency when used in different locations.
7. They can be effective with seasonal and everyday products.
8. They appeal to consumers' desire to save money and time.

How to Use for Best Results

1. Choose related products.
2. Choose products that are easily picked up.
3. Choose products that are relatively low priced.
4. Combine impulse items with needed items.
5. Keep the racks in high-traffic, high-visibility locations.
6. Use signs to increase sense of urgency.

Stack Displays

What It Is

Stack displays consist of any display where the merchandise is simply stacked on the sales floor. It can include products in boxes, bags or nested together (such as trash cans.) It is one of the easiest display methods to use.

Why Stack Displays Work

1. They bring excitement and urgency to large items and big-ticket merchandise.
2. They put lots of product in a small amount of space.
3. They focus consumer attention on the product
4. They create an image of value.
5. They enhance a store's price image.
6. They require no special fixtures, although platforms could be used.
7. They appeal to consumers' desire to save money and time.
8. They put excitement in shopping.

How to Use Stack Displays for Best Results

1. Choose bagged or boxed items.
2. Use colorful packaging to catch attention.
3. Choose unpackaged items that stack conveniently.
4. Choose items that require assembling and set them up.
5. Choose seasonal items for special promotions.
6. Tie in displays with advertised specials.

Vignettes

What It Is

A Vignette (also called a store-within-a-store display) presents products the way consumers want to buy them. Vignettes add color and interest and enhance your store image. Vignettes sell more than merchandise; they sell ideas and the desire to own by simulating a home setting.

Why Vignettes Work

1. How-to merchandising gives customers ideas and suggestions on how to carry out the ideas.
2. These displays show customers how they can use products at home or show how the products will look in their home.

How to Use Vignettes for Best Results

1. You can combine merchandise from several departments and make the merchandise easy to see and touch.
2. Vignette displays are more relaxed than packaged merchandise on shelves.
3. Create a miniroom with two adjacent walls that incorporate a faux finish technique, window treatments, area rug, lighting, chair-rail molding, furniture, and other home decor accessories.

Cross Merchandising

What It Is

Cross merchandising is when you display products together that are used together in projects. This is especially effective for related items normally stocked in different departments. Cross-aisle merchandising is displaying related merchandise on facing shelves.

Why Cross Merchandising Works

1. Customers want convenience and one-stop shopping.
2. Cross merchandising suggests related items.

3. It organizes products the way they are used.
4. It can suggest better quality items.
5. It appeals to consumers' desire to save time.
6. It makes shopping easier.
7. It gives customers project information.

How to Use for Best Results

1. Look for opportunities to combine products from different departments.
2. Take advantage of seasonal projects.
3. Promote common household repair and maintenance projects.
4. Display the pairs in the department where customers are most likely to go first.
5. Look for vendor planograms that take advantage of cross merchandising.
6. Use informative signing to compare benefits of good-better-best quality and remind customers of items that complete projects.

Some Good Products to Cross Merchandise Together

1. Electric trimmers and extension cords
2. Lawn sprinklers and garden hose
3. Plungers and liquid drain cleaners
4. Garden gloves and shovels
5. Batteries and flashlights

Other fixtures you may find on the sales floor include the following:

Acrylic trays. These are also referred to as shelf fixtures and are typically used to build cosmetic sets.

4-Way. A four-sided fixture used in Action Alleys to feature merchandise. It can be pegged or shelved, modularized, or flex.

Floor Display. A freestanding display of merchandise that sits on the sales floor.

Island Display. Island-type display used to hold products in the middle of the store stacked alone, either in a floor display, or on a table.

Pallet. Some stores use regular wooden pallets to stack merchandise on.

Spinner Rack. This is a fixture that rotates around for the customer to view product.

CHAPTER 7

Resets

In This Chapter

❖ Understanding a POG
❖ Understanding a Shelf Report
❖ Reset Step-by-Step Instructions

Resets are the next step up in merchandising work. Resets are the total makeover of a category. A Category is the grouping of products that have a common consumer end use; i.e., pet foods, laundry soap, oral care, foot care, paper towels, baking, etc. You will be moving products to align with a new authorized and approved layout by using a planogram. You will be cleaning the fixtures and placing new labels.

Sometimes resets are avoided because they are physically and mentally demanding. But resets are where the money is! Don't let resets scare you. Yes, they are time consuming and demand all of your attention, but they are also one of the most rewarding tasks of merchandising work. In this chapter, we will go through the basics of resets so you will know what they are and you will have the basic knowledge of how to complete one.

Knowing how to read and implement a POG is one of the most important skills a merchandiser needs to have. It is not difficult to learn how to read and work with POGs, and once you have mastered this skill, it will make your work far easier and rewarding.

A POG (i.e., POG, Plannagram, Plan-O-gram, Schematic, Modular, or MOD) is a diagram showing the exact location of each product on a shelf/fixture/display.

A POG is a computerized blueprint developed at a store's headquarters. It is designed to ensure two things:

1. Retailer has the desired product displayed to the customer.
2. The optimal inventory is on each shelf after the merchandiser sets the display.

This is the roadmap to your final destination, so it is essential to have the proper POG.

POGs are broken down into categories and then sections within a department. A Category is the grouping of products that have a common consumer end use, e.g., pet foods, laundry soap, oral care, foot care, paper towels, baking, etc. A Section is a specific kind of product or brand of product broken down into usually a four-foot section.

POGs are usually set in four-foot sections with the following listings:

1. Each box on the POG represents a product facing. The number of the same product facing the customer on the shelf, fixture, or display is the total count of facings.
2. Numbers on the product facings are referred to as Loc IDs.
3. Loc IDs cross-reference the schematic to the SKU Stock-Keeping Unit) Listings.
4. The SKU Listings give more information about each product.

Components of a POG

1. Cover Page—Some companies list the following on a cover page; others list these on the schematic page.

    a. Instructions
    b. Fixture accessories
    c. Signing
    d. Point of Purchase (POP) materials

2. Schematic—All POGs will have a schematic.

a. Show the set date.

b. A computerized drawing of the POG, showing all the details to set it accurately.

c. The number of shelves and peg hooks you will need (this should be the same on your POG as they are at the store unless you are adding/deleting shelving or the length is expanding or decreasing).

d. The width, depth, and height of the section (this also should be the same on the POG as they are at the store unless the section length/height is expanding or decreasing).

e. Details about the product placement.

f. Occasionally, the placement of promotional materials.

g. Shelf heights are sometimes included in the POG. Check existing shelf heights with a tape measure and make sure they are the same as the POG. Do this by measuring the airspace (or elevation) between the shelves. (It is important to remember that each chain measures the airspace between their shelves differently. Some measure the distance from the top of a shelf to the bottom of the shelf above it. This is called Top to Bottom. Others measure the distance from the top of a shelf to the top of the shelf above it. This is called Top to Top. If in doubt of how your store measures their shelf heights, check with the department manager or your supervisor for more details.)

h. Sometimes "product flow" or "traffic flow" is included on the POG. The product flow is based on the planned traffic movement of consumers through a specific department or the store. Most POGs read from left to right unless it specifies "Mirror Image." If it is a "Mirror Image," it is read backward, from Right to Left. Many POGs will have an arrow on the lower left-hand corner of the schematic that shows which direction a POG should be set. This arrow is called the lead-in arrow. Setting a POG with a lead in can get a little tricky, so understanding the concepts are very important. When setting a POG with a lead in arrow, you will need to be aware of the location of the gondola in relation to the main aisle. It is important to ask store personnel where the main aisles are.

Now let's take a look at a sample planogram and see what kind of information it gives us.

TLOW Candy Gum&Mints Energy Shot Btm 3ftx54in

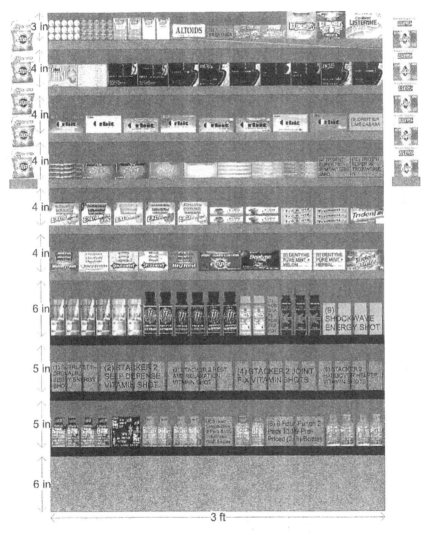

Traffic N/A

TLOW Candy Gum&Mints Energy Shot Btm 3ftx54in

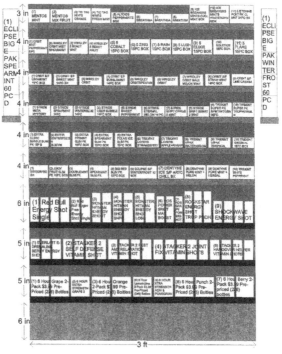

Traffic N/A

Shelf Report

The shelf report is sometimes attached to the POG. It provides a full description of the product with a corresponding number of the order they should be placed on the shelf. When reading the shelf report, it is important to remember that the bottom shelf of the left section is usually shelf 1. Product position number one is the farthest to the left on shelf number 1.

The shelf report includes a list of new and discontinued items. On some POGs, deletions are shown as shelf 0.

The POG and the shelf report both provide the same information, only in different formats. On a shelf report, facings are more visible and easier to see; therefore, many merchandisers actually prefer using it instead of a POG.

Shelf 0.1

	UPC	Eby Num	Pack Size	Name	Facings
1	223190	636167	4	ECLIPSE BIG E PAK SPEARMINT 60 PC D 4.00...	1

Shelf 0.11

	UPC	Eby Num	Pack Size	Name	Facings
1	223170	636175	4	ECLIPSE BIG E PAK WINTERFROST 60 PC D 4...	1

Shelf 1.2

	UPC	Eby Num	Pack Size	Name	Facings
1	7811400367	DSD	6	6 HOUR GRAPE 2-PACK $3.99 PRE-PRICED (2...	2
2	78114004036	DSD	0	6 HOUR EXTRA STRENGTH GRAPE 2 2.00 OZ	1
3	7811400377	DSD	6	6 HOUR ORANGE 2-PACK $3.99 PRE-PRICED ...	2
4	7811400387	DSD	6	6 HOUR LEMON-LIME 2-PACK $3.99 PRE-PRIC...	1
5	78114005170	DSD	0	6 HOUR XTRA STRENGTH ACAI & POMEGRA...	1
6	7811400392	DSD	6	6 HOUR PUNCH 2-PACK $3.99 PRE-PRICED (2...	2
7	7811400372	DSD	6	6 HOUR BERRY 2-PACK $3.99 PRE-PRICED (2...	2

Shelf 1.3

	UPC	Eby Num	Pack Size	Name	Facings
1	9473400206	DSD	6	EVERLAST E-DRENALINE BERRY ENERGY S...	3
2	7811400634	DSD	12	STACKER 2 SELF DEFENSE VITAMIN SHOT 1...	4
3	7811400601	DSD	12	STACKER 2 REST AND RELAXATION VITAMIN...	4
4	7811400595	DSD	12	STACKER 2 JOINT FIX VITAMIN SHOTS 12.00 ...	5
5	7811400598	DSD	12	STACKER 2 HANGOVER HELPER VITAMIN SH...	4

Shelf 1.4

	UPC	Eby Num	Pack Size	Name	Facings
1	1126939444	DSD	12	RED BULL ENERGY SHOT SINGLE 12.00 CT	4
2	1126939445	DSD	12	RED BULL SUGAR FREE ENERGY SHOT SING...	2
3	7084788050	DSD	24	MONSTER HITMAN ENERGY SHOOT 3.00 OZ	2
4	7084788056	DSD	24	MONSTER HITMAN ENERGY SHOT SNPR 3.00...	2
5	7084788061	DSD	24	MONSTER HITMAN ENERGY SHOT LOBO 3.00...	2
6	8079380609	DSD	12	NOS POWER SHOT MAX BOOST 2.00 OZ	2
7	80793806638	DSD	12	NOS GRAPE POWERSHOT 2.00 OZ	1
8	1809400910	DSD	12	ROCKSTAR ENERGY SHOT TROP PNCH 2.50 ...	3
9	5239700004	DSD	12	SHOCKWAVE ENERGY SHOT 2.00 OZ	4

Shelf 1.5

	UPC	Eby Num	Pack Size	Name	Facings
1	229680	025544	10	WINTERFRESH SLIM PK 15PC BOX 10.00 CT	1
2	229130	010793	10	JUICY FRUIT SLIM PK 15PC BOX 10.00 CT	1
3	229120	010785	10	DOUBLEMINT SLIM PK 15PC BOX 10.00 CT	1
4	229110	010777	10	SPEARMINT SLIM PK 15PC BOX 10.00 CT	1
5	229650	010769	10	BIG RED SLIM PK 15PC BOX 10.00 CT	1
6	229080	265918	12	ECLIPSE S/F WINTERFROST 12 BOX 12.00 CT	1
7	1254630059	068437	12	DENTYNE ICE S/F ARTC CHILL BX 12.00 CT	1
8	1254630805	776278	10	DENTYNE PURE MINT + MELON 10.00 CT	1
9	1254630801	776260	10	DENTYNE PURE MINT + HERBAL 10.00 CT	1
10	1254661752	343491	12	TRIDENT WHITE PEPPRMNT 12PC BOX 12.00 ...	1

Shelf 1.6

	UPC	Eby Num	Pack Size	Name	Facings
1	229190	017061	10	EXTRA CLSSC BUBBLE SLIM PK 15P B 10.00 CT	1
2	229180	011486	10	EXTRA WINTERFRESH SLIM PK 15PC B 10.00 ...	1
3	228910	010876	10	EXTRA PPRMNT SLIM PK 15PC BOX 10.00 CT	1
4	228990	010694	10	EXTRA SPEARMINT SLIM PK 15PC BOX 10.00 ...	1
5	228980	068148	10	EXTRA POLAR ICE SLIM PK 15PC BOX 10.00 CT	1

Resets are the total makeover of a category. Knowing the difference between a POG reset and a POG revision will save you lots of time. A revision means you will only remove certain products and replace them with new ones. **You will always change the shelf labels**. It also means you will not have to take down the entire POG and rebuild it, saving valuable time. Study your instructions; they will tell you if the change is a reset or a revision. You will be moving products to align with a new POG and cleaning the fixtures and placing new labels. They are time-consuming and physically and mentally demanding. Resets are also one of the most rewarding tasks of merchandising work. Just seeing where I started from and what the product looks like is so fulfilling! Although the biggest reward is that resets are where the money is!

Reset Instructions: One Step at a Time

Prep Work

Step 1. At least one week before the reset, go through the instructions and call your supervisor with any questions.

Step 2. Precall the store to set up a date for the reset and confirm they have received the fixtures and supplies you will need. Sometimes the fixtures and supplies will be sent directly to you. Let them know if you will need additional shelving, and ask if it will be available. Request a tag run so they will be ready for your reset. Most stores can print labels on location, but others must order from the main office, so make sure you give enough advance notice so the store can have your labels ready by the scheduled reset date. Stores can print out a copy of their current store specific POG if needed. Ask when the employees are allowed to enter the store and if you may enter with them, even before the store opens. That way you will not be interrupted as much by customers or be in the customers' way.

The Reset

Step 1. Arrive at the store as early as possible. When it comes to resets, the main word in clothing is "comfortable." That does not mean "anything goes." You will still be held to neat and clean but not to professional attire.

1. Put on your company-supplied name tag identifying yourself as a merchandiser.
2. Sign into the Vendor's Log noting the time. The Vendor's Log is usually located at customer service or in the receiving area.
3. Get a cart to use as a portable workspace.

Before you start

Step 1. Proceed to Department.

1. Check in with the department manager and confirm you are there to do the reset.

a. Ask them for the labels if any new fixtures/supplies were sent to the store and where the new product is located.

b. This would also be a good time to verify how the **Deletes** (i.e., Disco'd or Discontinued items) are to be handled. Check with store personnel about obtaining containers to store-deleted and back-stocked items.

c. Ask your department manager any questions you may have regarding the reset. If needed, call your supervisor. They can return your call at the store if necessary.

2. Survey the area that you will be working in and compare to your instructions and POG. It is highly recommended to analyze a set thoroughly before starting. Sometimes you can remove just some of the merchandise to make room to execute the new planogram. This means there is less merchandise in the cart or on the floor. Remember to clean the shelf. It may be like a lot of the cosmetic resets where just a few items are pull and plug or just two sections of the set are changing. Why do more then we have to?

3. Check the length and size of your set to the POG and ensure you have the correct POG. When working a major reset, keep the sections' POG taped to the corresponding section. There is nothing worse than grabbing up the wrong sections' POG and placing product. Later you might find you must remove the product because you used the wrong POG for that section. Unless the set is increasing or decreasing in length or size, the POG and set should match.

4. Check the number of shelves on the POG against the number that is actually there. Unless you are adding shelves, these should match your POG. Make sure you have the correct size shelving before you start removing product. If shelf heights are included in the POG, check existing shelf heights with a tape measure and make sure they are the same as the POG. If you are working a tight airspace set, one wrong shelf height could mess up your whole reset. If the actual shelving heights are different from on the POG, you will be adjusting the shelving as you go to match the POG. This is done to accommodate height of product.

5. To check existing shelf heights, use a tape measure to verify if shelves will be moving before you start to set product. Do this by measuring the airspace (or elevation) between the shelves. (Remember that each chain measures the airspace between their shelves differently. Some will be "top to bottom," some "top to top." See Components

of a Planogram, Sec. 2g.) Only adjust shelving after comparing the existing shelf measurements to the shelf heights listed on the POG.

6. **What if the store set does not match the footage of the POG?** First, consult with the department manager for their recommendations. If you must expand the footage, use double facings of store brands and top-selling products. If your store does not have enough space for the smallest POG you have, then you must reduce the footage of your set. Begin by removing all the deletes first and then reduce the number of facings until your set will fit the stores' footage. Consult your department manager as to which products' facings should be reduced or doubled.

7. If you are setting a combination shelf/peg hook POG, set the shelves first from the bottom up and then set the peg hooks from the top down. Adjust where needed. There are varieties of peg hooks, J-Hooks, Skyhooks, etc. Always have the correct number of Peg Hooks/J-hooks and holders before you start. Make sure you have the correct peg hooks for the POG. Pegs hooks come in different shapes, sizes, and lengths. Always make sure to use the correct size peg hook.

8. Check the "product flow" on the POG.

9. Sometimes when doing a reset, very little product is being moved. So before you start pulling product off the shelf, look over the POG to get a "feel" for how much of the set is moving.

10. Remember to keep product, cleaning supplies, and additional shelving out of the main aisles and away from customers. It is your responsibility to keep the work area safe and shoppable.

In reset work, it is neither best to be the hare nor the turtle. Yes, you need to work fast, but not so fast that you make costly mistakes that take a lot of time to go back and fix. The best pace is a steady and methodical pace that helps you stay accurate in the work that you do. It is better to work smart than fast and have to go back to fix errors.

Step 2

If store personnel have not already pulled deleted/discontinued product, pull it and place it in the designated container. When removing deletes from the set, it makes a difference if the deletes are vendor direct-store-delivery (DSD) items or items that a warehoused at the store's distribution center. As discussed previously in "All about Labels," this information may be right on the label for the product. Box these deletes separately depending on which one it is.

Always mark the box, basket, or cart with what's inside, such as backstock, deletes to vendor or return center, non-POG product (product that is neither an authorized return or on the POG), etc. This helps everyone, including you, keep organized.

Returns are deleted items that are returnable. Returns are products that are authorized to be sent back to the vendor or warehouse for reimbursement. The product may be damaged, is no longer carried by the store, or is excess stock.

Setting a POG during store hours can be a formidable task. In most cases, you will have customers making purchases off the POG that you are working on; therefore, it is best to keep the area as shoppable as possible. Many stores will want you to work in four-foot sections versus resetting the entire POG at one time. If you are resetting the POG after the store's closing, it may be easier to set all sections at the same time.

If after reviewing the POG you find this is a major reset, where the majority of the product is moving to a new home, then start working in the bottom left corner and clear a three—or four-foot section. Remove all products that will remain with the POG reset and group it on the side of the aisle. Place the product in a cart with the existing label attached to the top of one of the items. Try keeping the same product items together as it will make putting them back on the shelf easier.

Moving lots of product to carts and then having to find them again to place on the shelf is handling the product more than needed. It is best to start with one four-foot section, clear it, and start placing product on it according to the POG. Leaving product on the shelf until you are ready to place it in its new home makes it easier to find, and you will be handling it only one time from its old to new home on the shelf. Handling the product only one time is working smarter and more time conscious.

Keep your holding carts to a minimum. This keeps the aisle open for customers to move about and shop. Some stores will only allow one holding cart on the sales floor at a time. If this is the case, you may have to move extra carts to the backroom while you work. Of course, sometimes moving lots of product to carts is necessary because shelf heights need adjusting or whole sections are moving.

If this is the case, pull a "set" of each SKU and set aside in a separate cart for that section. Pull the rest of the product neatly into shopping carts keeping SKUs together. You can layer different products in a cart for holding, but never overfill your cart. When a product is needed to fill the shelf, it will surely be the one buried beneath multiple layers of other product. Also, never pile product on the floor. Carts hold excess product.

Clean the empty shelf or fixture first before reloading product. Always clean shelves and shelf tag channels as needed. Use a good cleaner and use your protective wear if applicable. Only use store-approved cleaning products, preferably theirs.

Install the new fixtures and/or peg hooks if applicable. On shelving that has bent or misaligned shelf brackets causing the shelf to hang lower than it should, use a penny on the back wall where the bracket goes into the upright bar on the shelving unit. There is enough weight to hold the penny in place and hold up the shelf so it lines nicely with its neighboring shelf.

When setting a POG with peg hooks, take the time to count the holes on the pegboard correctly. Either the peg holes will appear on the schematic, or measurements will appear on the line listing that give you inches up from the base and inches over from the lead in.

When doing pegged resets like cosmetics, you should get some empty peg hooks from the store (if the hooks are not vendor provided). When pulling the product from its old home, leave the product on its peg hook so that it is easier to find and to place in its new spot or to keep it together for a return-to-vendor. This saves time because again you are handling the product less. Use the additional empty peg hooks for new product that has not yet arrived at the store.

When doing a lot of pegboard resets such as cosmetics, some merchandisers purchase a piece of pegboard to use just for these types of sets. When removing a peg during a reset, they place the pegs with product on the pegboard to keep things orderly and easy to return to the new POG/modular location.

If working with carded product and the peg hole tears, use a repair tab. If neither you nor the store has them, try using the store's staple gun to salvage the peg hole. The staple will hold up to the weight of the product much better than placing tape over the hole.

If there is a shelf above the peg section, set that shelf after the pegs are set with at least one item on each peg. The reason is that many times pegs have to be readjusted and you need that space above to move and fix the peg hooks.

Remove stickers, price tags, and POP materials, and be sure you do not destroy POP materials that may be reused. Do not skip this step unless directed by store personnel. *Do not* take any old fixtures / old labels, etc., to the dumpster at this point. Keep all this in a separate waiting cart until you have completed the reset and all-new fixtures/labels are in place. From experience, I can assure you that, at some point, you will be digging through the old fixtures to reuse one after you find out the store did not receive one of the new fixtures or pulling an old label to reuse until the store can print a new one.

Most POGs will tell you where to set the shelves' height above the base either by inches or by notches along the side. You will need to count these to set the shelf correctly. Usually the height indicated is the top of the shelf. Work each section separately. Start on bottom shelf, and work up one shelf at a time. Please remember that line item numbers start on the left and move right.

Before filling in the POG with product, place all the point-of-purchase materials or additional signing on the POG.

Start loading the product according to the POG left to right, unless otherwise noted, into the first section that you have cleared. Work the row length to the end of the set. Using the "set" of each SKU that you set aside, place one unit of each product on the shelf or peg hook for each facing listed on the POG to ensure that SKU will fit. If the product does not fit, you need to adjust the shelves. Once those are in place, you can fill the shelf with the rest of the product from the shopping carts.

Just a little side comment. Ever wonder about the theory behind product placement? We read left to right, so it is assumed the last thing the customer sees on the right they will purchase. So, bigger sizes of product are to the right of smaller sizes. Also, the same principle applies to private store brands. They are always placed to the right of national brands of corresponding sizes. This is called, "The store brand rule".

Use a pencil and check off the item as you set it. When you start reading your POG again, you will know where you left off. And then as I mark product off on the shelf report or POG, I circle the items that need a label. Then when I am done with the set, I have all the products needing labels right in front of me.

When I do mess up, like leave out a facing as I set (which happens more times than I want to admit) I can fix my error earier by using an 18 inch ruler or something like a paint stirring stick to move the product over and cut in a space for a product that I missed. Works real handy when working with smaller items like vitamins or small boxed items.

Continue to move up one shelf at a time, working each shelf in the same way. You should never deviate from the POG. If a section cannot be set according to POG for any reason, you must first discuss the options with a supervisor or store manager before proceeding. If there are issues with fit, have the store personnel make adjustments to ensure the fit of each product.

When you come to a new product that the store does not have yet, you need to leave the appropriate amount of space for the new product. A quick trick is to place the correct number of facings of a similar-sized product on the shelf backward as a "spacer." This way your spacing doesn't get off. When you are done with the reset, you can visually identify the "spacers" representing the new product and tag as though the new product was on the shelf. Place your "spacers" back in their proper position when done.

JUDITH ADKINS-SPEARS

Always match the product, as you place it, to the UPC or store's item number supplied on the POG and/or shelf label to ensure you are placing the correct product in the correct space. Never go by description alone. You don't need to check the whole UPC or store's item number—just the last three numbers for verification will do. As you work, you can mark the items off the POG as you place them on the shelf. Make a special marking on the POG for shelf labels that are missing. Then when you are done, you can easily find the ones that need tags.

When you do remove product from its old home, always keep the shelf label with the product. Keep the existing labels that you have with the product as you move it into its new location. It helps to find it later when you are looking for that one item.

If you have new labels, the store usually wants them placed, instead of using the old labels. Labels are usually placed on the shelf molding just below the product justified on the left-hand side of the first facing. Check with your particular store for proper placement of the label.

If you have missing/damaged labels, and the store cannot supply printed labels, you will have to handwrite labels. Get blank tags from the department manager. Most stores require the following info on the tag: description, UPC number, their item or stocking code number, and price. You can then place the tag in the appropriate space. After all changes have been made and all products are placed on the shelf, place labels correctly according to the POG. Decide what labels are missing and ask store personnel for new labels. You will usually place labels under the left-hand edge of the product.

Find out if there is Point of Purchase (POP) needed for this POG. Typically, the POP material or any additional signing needs will be listed on the cover page and/or schematic page. Before filling in the POG with product, place all the point-of-purchase materials or additional signing on the POG. Once all products, labels, and POP materials fit, it is time to fill in the POG with stock.

Put any excess product into containers to go to the stockroom. If there is product missing from the POG, you can have store personnel bring additional product from the stock areas to fill in. Break down boxes as you go. Ask store personnel where to take boxes.

Clean up your work area. Return any cleaning materials supplied by the store. Make sure you leave nothing behind. Check that debris and supplies have been removed from the aisle. Throw away any trash; put back any unused shelves, pegs, etc. Take any garbage to the dumpster.

Give the deletes to the department manager or take to the claims department as instructed. Authorized returns may require a **Return Authorization (RA) number**. The **claims clerk** needs this particular number to process a return. Your numbers for returning any product will be included in your instructions. Bring discontinued, damaged, and outdated merchandise to the attention of store management for disposition. When handling damaged goods or returns, be certain to follow the store's specific procedures on where to put the merchandise and how to box it. **Never take any product home with you**.

If you are working on a merchandising team, have the lead person of your team check your finished POG. Make any necessary adjustments.

Ask the Department Manager if the reset meets their approval. Then have them or the Store Manager sign your paperwork and get a store stamp if required by your company. If necessary, ask the Department Manager where the stamp is located. It is usually in the claims department or the store manager's office.

On your way out of the store, sign out of the vendor's log by noting the time you leave.

After Completion

On the same day, report project completions. Complete reports for each job, each day. Know how your company handles reports and the period you have to get the report in to your company. Most companies require you to confirm the work you have done by using a voicemail system, an online web form, or fax. To confirm you have called in, a confirmation number or payment authorization number is given that you will write on forms.

Merchandisers must call low/out of stocks or missing fixtures/supplies orders to the individual companies that supply the store. Finish filling out your project forms, activity reports, and time sheets and then mail promptly. In some cases, you must also forward odometer readings and reimbursable expenses with receipts to the company.

Reporting

Company Headquarters uses the information that you provide to ensure the stores are complying with company, state, and federal regulations, store promotions, etc. Failure to provide accurate information could jeopardize scores as well as the continued contract with the client.

There are several ways to get information from the office to the field, from the field to the office and feedback from the office to the client. Reporting from any source must contain all pertinent information. Some companies fax or mail paperwork, while others have web-based reporting systems, Interactive Voice Response (IVR), e-mail, computerized voice mail systems, or handheld pocket PCs or laptops. Although there are many avenues that transport reports, the information contained in the reports is standard.

The client and the company agree on the merchandising project. The company needs to distribute the information to the merchandiser, either directly to the merchandiser or through the supervisor. As the merchandiser completes the assignment, the reporting process continues.

Information contained in the report is the **date**, **job identification**, **merchandiser identification, and client or product identification**, **start and end time**, questions **pertaining to the particular project**, and **room for comments.** Store management will sign or stamp this report.

If this information is handwritten, it is very important that it be legible and organized. Reporting is a necessary part of every job, and it is very important to keep this information neat and organized. The client reviews information gathered from your reports.

How You Can Prevent Incorrect Reporting!

1   Familiarize yourself with your assignments prior to starting the cycle, and organize your paperwork prior to entering the stores. This will ensure that you are able to complete all the work during your visit and provide accurate data for the clients.
2   Write down the store number on each worksheet that you take into the store. Another idea is to use a different-colored pen or highlighter for each specific store.
3   Double-check the store number on the Sign Off sheet with management when they are signing the form.
4   When you are entering the information on the computer, verify that you are entering the correct information for each store by reviewing the information on the store's sign off sheet.
5   If you make an error and didn't catch it before the information was sent, contact your DM immediately! Changes can be submitted before the final report is sent in.

Reset Tools

These were discussed in an earlier section, but I cannot emphasize enough the importance of having the right tool for the job. At one time or another, I have needed every one of these tools on a reset. When you are in the middle of a reset, there is no time to start searching for tools that you need. Having these ready to use at any reset will save you a lot of time.

- **Label Peeler.** Label peelers help lift existing labels off the shelf and make it easier on your fingers and nails. If your company doesn't supply one, try a plastic grapefruit peeler.
- **Ruler or Yardstick cut to eighteen inches.** Use this to easily straighten product on the shelf or to push over small items in the set.
- **Tape Measure.** Use to measure shelving heights and lengths.
- **Sharpie Fine Tip felt pen.** If you need to handwrite labels, this type of pen would work on all types of label paper.
- **Large Felt Pen marker (like a *Marks-A-Lot* marker).** Use to write disco'd or overstock on boxes containing deleted or overstock product.
- **Wet Ones.** Use for a quick wash for your hands as you will get filthy when doing a reset.

- **Garbage Bag.** Grab a plastic bag or paper bag from the front register to put all your accumulated garbage in.
- **Cleaning Supplies.** Use the store's cleaning spray and paper towels. Get these from the front registers or the department manager.
- **Store-approved scratcher/scrapper.** You will not believe the goop and crud that will be stuck to the shelves!
- **Hammer (Regular and Rubber).** To be used where stubborn shelves must be moved.
- **Box cutter/knife.** Very helpful when opening multiple boxes of new product.
- **Screwdrivers.** Always a good idea to have a Phillips and regular.
- **Pliers.** Straighten bent fixtures, shelving, and whatever else.
- **Step stool.** You can usually use the store's step stool, but there is no guarantee they will have what you need.
- **Small Paintbrush.** Use a one-fourth—to one-half-inch-wide paintbrush to clean dust and dirt out of crevices.

What if the reset took a different amount of time to complete than the companies' time limit? Usually you claim the allowed time for the reset even if it took less time. Talk to you supervisor if you have more questions about this. Reset estimated times are based on a physical "test set." A test set will also include a "fit check" to take place to assure that everything fits properly in the section. These physical tests' times can be a bit misleading. The test sets are done in a controlled environment—no customers shopping the aisle, no broken or dirty fixtures and shelving that need cleaned or fixed, or a store that makes additional requirements on the merchandiser before they approve the set, etc. Some of the estimates of time given are nothing more than wishful thinking on the client's part. So keep track of the time you are spending on a reset. If you are getting close to the time limit and expect that you will need additional time to complete, call your supervisor. Be prepared to explain the additional time (i.e., extra time cleaning extremely dirty fixtures, extra time locating fixtures/supplies, customized set, had to pull additional nonplanogrammed items, had to handwrite missing tags, etc.). Each reset or client job will present its own set of "special" circumstances, but if you are working for a good merchandising company, they will compensate you for any out of the ordinary circumstances.

CHAPTER 8

Workplace Safety

In This Chapter

❖ Slips, Trips, and Falls
❖ Lifting Injuries
❖ Safety Guidelines for Hand
❖ Safety Guidelines for Power Tools
❖ Safe Driving Tips
❖ Driving in Fog
❖ Winter Driving Tips
❖ Driving in the Rain

Accident prevention is a basic requirement of your position as a merchandiser. You will be held accountable for unsafe behavior. It is the responsibility of each merchandiser to accept and follow their company's established safety regulations and procedures. Working safely is a requirement of the job. Merchandisers are expected to assist management in accident-prevention activities. Unsafe conditions must be reported immediately. No employees are expected to work in an unsafe environment.

Most people blame accidents on unsafe conditions. But in truth, most accidents are caused by unsafe behaviors. The best way to eliminate accidents is to avoid unsafe practices. Housekeeping is a continuous process needed to keep the workplace free of debris and other hazards while putting all things in their proper place. Periodic inspections should be performed to review housekeeping practices and identify workplace hazards. It is the responsibility of every employee to observe good housekeeping practices at all times. Some housekeeping tips are as follows:

1. Keep work areas clean and orderly. Totes, bunkers (carts), flattops, and other equipment must be pushed to one side of the aisle while you are working. The aisle must be open to customers and easily accessible.
2. Store all tools, equipment, and supplies in their proper place. When a box cutter is not in use, the blade must be kept in the closed position, locked with the guard in place. Razor blades are strictly prohibited.
3. Wipe up all spills or notify your supervisor if additional help is needed.
4. Place trash in the proper trash containers. Boxes should be placed beside the baler, not inside the baler.
5. Do not stack totes more than four high. When a tote is full, place it out of the aisle in its designated storage area. Use dollies or flattops to transport heavier totes or more than one at a time. Keep your back straight while you are pushing a dolly. Hold the handle with one hand and place the other hand on the top tote for balance. Do not overload hand dollies or flattops; ask for assistance.

Some of the more common accidents in the retail business include the following:

1. Falling on a slippery surface or stairs
2. Lifting injuries
3. Falling from a ladder or chair
4. Tripping on a rough surface
5. Sprains and strains
6. Cutting injuries (box cutters)

Slips, Trips, and Falls

Slips, trips, and falls are the third leading cause of injuries to employees. These are among the most serious accidents that occur in retail stores and similar work environments. Some precautions include the following:

1. Wearing proper shoes that enable you to move comfortably and maintain firm footing—open-toed shoes or sandals are not acceptable. Make sure the soles of the shoes are designed for the surface you are working on. The wrong type of sole can actually add to the hazards you face on the job.

2. Be aware of floor surfaces; clean up spills as soon as possible. If you fail to clean it up or notify someone that the spill exists, someone else may slip and fall.
3. Know the clean up procedure for chemical spills.
4. *Don't* run.

Lifting Injuries

Improper lifting is the greatest single cause of back pain and injury, so it is important that merchandisers learn and practice good lifting techniques. Remember, if you think you need help in lifting, make sure you ask for it!

Lifting Information—Did You Know?

• Lifting causes three out of every four back injuries.
• Back injuries can disable you for life; luckily, they are almost always preventable.

How Can You Stay Safe?

Stretch your muscles. Stretching prepares your body for the lift. You wouldn't play a sport without stretching; you shouldn't lift without stretching either. Size up the load. If it looks too heavy or awkward to carry alone, then ask for help. Take distance into consideration because objects feel heavier the longer you hold on to them.

Proper Lifting Techniques

1. Stand close to the object you are lifting and plant both feet firmly on the floor, about shoulder width apart. Point your toes out.
2. Squat down close to the object with your back straight, knees bent, and stomach muscles tight.
3. Grip the object firmly with both hands, not just your fingers.
4. Stand up slowly, keeping your back straight and letting your legs do the lifting.
5. Avoid bending from the waist. Keep your knees bent and back straight when lifting from the ground.
6. Reverse the above procedures to put the load down.

7. Don't jump! A jump from a short height (such as the back of a trailer or loading dock) can cause serious injury.

Unloading Trailers

1. Use a stepladder to gain access to the trailer—never use a pallet as a ladder.
2. Watch for improperly stacked items; they may become falling objects.
3. Do not jump down from the back of the trailer. Use a ladder.

Safety Checklist

1. Don't overestimate your own strength.
2. Walk, don't run, to prevent slips and falls.
3. Use equipment—hand trucks, dollies versus lifting when possible.
4. Break a large load into smaller loads.
5. Remove any objects you might trip over.
6. Check the object you'll be carrying for rough or jagged edges.
7. Make sure the moving equipment works properly before using it to move product.
8. Change your working positions frequently. (Chronic strain due to an unchanging work position can weaken your back, arms, and shoulders.)
9. Adjust working heights to prevent slumping or excessive reaching.
10. Stretch during the day to increase your flexibility.
11. Take body relaxation breaks. Let your shoulders and neck muscles go limp, swivel your head or arms, flex your hands and fingers.
12. Wear gloves with a good grip.
13. Wear safety shoes with reinforced toes and nonskid soles.
14. Push—don't pull if the load is too heavy or too large.
15. Have a first aid kit in an accessible location.
16. If you are taking medications, then be aware of its effect on performance and take precautions.
17. Do not work if you are ill or impaired by fatigue.
18. Ask your coworkers for assistance.

Safety Guidelines for Hand and Power Tools

Appropriate personal protective equipment should be worn due to hazards that may be encountered while using portable power tools and hand tools.

- Be aware of your environment, paying close attention to power lines and electrical circuits, water pipes, and other mechanical hazards, particularly those below the work surface, hidden from your view, which may be contacted.
- All observers should be kept at a safe distance away from the work area.

Hand Tool Safety Guidelines

The greatest hazards posed by hand tools result from misuse and improper maintenance. Here are some examples:

1. Using a screwdriver as a chisel may cause the tip of the screwdriver to break and fly, hitting the user or other employees.
2. If a wooden handle on a tool such as a hammer or an axe is loose, splintered, or cracked, the head of the tool may fly off and strike the user or another worker.
3. A wrench must not be used if its jaws are sprung because it might slip.
4. Impact tools such as chisels, wedges, or drift pins are unsafe if they have mushroomed heads. The heads might shatter on impact, sending sharp fragments flying.

Power Tool Safety Guidelines

All hazards involved in the use of power tools can be prevented by following basic safety rules:

1. Keep all tools in good condition with regular maintenance.
2. Use the right tool for the job.
3. Examine each tool for damage before use.
4. Operate according to the manufacturer's instructions.
5. Ground all tools unless double insulated.
6. Avoid accidental starting. Workers should not hold a finger on the switch button while carrying a plugged-in tool.
7. All portable electric tools that are damaged shall be removed from use and tagged Do Not Use.

8. When not in use, tools should be stored in a dry place.
9. Electric tools should not be used in damp or wet locations.
10. Unplug tools before installing, adjusting, and changing any accessory or attachment of any kind.
11. Drills: never force a drill. Apply enough pressure to keep the drill bit cutting smoothly. If the drill slows down, then relieve the pressure.

Driving

Safe Driving Tips: Driving and Cell Phones

1. Do not use a cell phone while driving *unless* you use a hands-free device. **(Some states require the use of a hands-free device when driving if using a cell phone. You must check and comply with the local state's law)**
2. Position your cell phone within easy reach.
3. Suspend conversations during hazardous driving conditions or situations.
4. Do not take notes or look up phone numbers while driving.
5. Dial sensibly and assess the traffic. Only place calls when you are not moving or before pulling into traffic.
6. Do not engage in stressful or emotional conversations that may be distracting.
7. Use your cell phone to call for help.
8. Use your cell phone to help others in emergencies.
9. Call roadside assistance or a special cell nonemergency assistance number when necessary.

Driving In Fog

The best advice we can give to drivers confronted with thick fog is to get off the road as soon as possible. If you can't or won't pull off the road, then we offer the following advice:

1. Keep your *minimum safety gap* to three seconds in ideal conditions; with the decreased visibility fog causes, this interval should be increased substantially.

2. Slow down. Most fog-related traffic fatalities occur because someone was driving too fast and couldn't stop in time to avoid a collision.
3. Make sure that you can be seen. Turn on your fog lights and use low beams. High beams direct light up into the fog, making it difficult for you to see. Low beams direct light down onto the road and help other drivers to see you.
4. If you leave the road, be sure to pull off completely. Turn off your driving lights and turn on your flashers so others know you're there but won't think you are driving on the road.
5. Always use your defroster and windscreen wipers in foggy conditions to keep the windows clear.
6. Keep an eye on your speedometer and maintain a slow, constant speed.
7. Remember that other drivers have a limited sight distance and that fog can leave roadways slick. Signal early, and when you use your brakes, don't stomp on them.

Winter Driving Tips

1. Before you shift into gear, plan the best route to your destination. Avoid hills and high-congestion areas.
2. Before you leave your driveway, scrape the ice and snow from every window and the exterior rear view mirrors, not just a small patch on the windshield. Don't forget to remove snow from headlights and brake lights.
3. Try to remove ice and snow from your shoes before getting in your vehicle. As they melt, they create moisture buildup, causing windows to fog on the inside. You can reduce this fogging by turning the air recirculation switch to the *off* position. This brings in drier, fresh air. You can also run your air conditioner, which serves as a dehumidifier for a few minutes.
4. You and your passengers must use safety belts, both lap and shoulder straps. Pull them snug to ensure they work properly.
5. Adjust headrests. Rear-end collisions are common in winter driving, and a properly-adjusted headrest can prevent or reduce neck injuries.
6. Before you shift into gear, plan the best route to your destination. Avoid hills, high-congestion areas and bridges if possible.
7. Although your radio can provide helpful traffic information, it can also be a distraction for some drivers. Since driving is more a mental skill than a physical skill, you may want to keep your radio turned off.

8. Don't use a cellular phone when driving on ice or snow. Even if you have a hands-free model, you need to concentrate on driving, not on a telephone conversation.

9. Drive slowly and remember that posted speed limits identify the maximum speed allowed when weather conditions are ideal. Law-enforcement agencies can write citations to motorists driving the posted speed limit if weather conditions warrant a slower speed.

10. Be more alert to the actions of other drivers.

11. Anticipate cars coming from side streets and put extra distance between your vehicle and the one in front of you. If someone is too close behind you, don't speed up; slow down or let them go around you.

12. To make sure other drivers see you, always drive with your lights on. At night, in fog and heavy snow conditions, low beams may be more effective than high beams.

13. Keep a light touch on the brakes. Even with antilock braking systems (sometimes called ABS) you should apply light pressure to avoid locking the brakes and causing a skid. Pumping the brake pedal should be smooth action, going from light to firm in a gradual move. Tip Toe to Slow is a good motto for winter drivers.

14. Keep both hands on the wheel and keep the wheel pointed where you want your car to go. While it may sound overly simple, it could help you in a skid. While manual transmissions may provide greater control to assist with braking, be careful when using downshifting as a way to slow the vehicle. Gear changes, particularly abrupt ones, can upset a vehicle's balance and cause a skid to occur, especially in turns.

Driving in the Rain

Losing control of your car on wet pavement is a frightening experience. Unfortunately, it can happen unless you take preventive measures.

If you do find yourself in a skid, remain calm

1. Ease your foot off the gas. Carefully steer in the direction you want the front of the car to go. To avoid hydroplaning:

   a. Keep your tires properly inflated.

b. Maintain good tread on your tires and replace them when necessary.
c. Slow down when roads are wet.
d. Stay away from puddles.
e. Try to drive in the tire tracks left by the cars in front of you.

If you find yourself hydroplaning

1. Do not brake or turn suddenly. This could throw your car into a skid.
2. Ease your foot off the gas until the car slows, and you can feel the road again.
3. If you need to brake, do it gently with light pumping actions. If your car has antilock brakes, then brake normally; the car's computer will mimic a pumping action when necessary.
4. A defensive driver adjusts his or her speed to the wet road conditions in time to avoid having to use any of these measures!

Tips for Drivers

1. Do not consume alcoholic beverages before or during driving.
2. **Always wear your seat belt**. Do not drive or move the vehicle until all your passengers buckle up.
3. Always drive within the speed limit.
4. Do not drive if you are fatigued. Alert your Branch Manager that another qualified driver must drive.
5. Tune your driving to the weather and time of day. You cannot drive in icy, wet, or dark conditions the same as you do in dry, light conditions.
6. Always use a spotter to help you back up.
7. Always give yourself plenty of time to arrive at your destination. Lateness does not give you an excuse to speed!
8. Periodically refresh your safe driving practices by rereading your Drivers' Training Materials.

Tips for Passengers

1. Always wear your seat belt. No excuses. You are twenty-five times more likely to die if you are ejected from a vehicle. Buckle up!

2. *Never* travel in a van or vehicle unless you have your own seat with your own seat belt. Do not sit on equipment, the floor, anyone's lap, or stretch out across other passengers.
3. Do not smoke.
4. Be a good passenger: courteous, quiet, and safe.
5. Speak up in the vehicle if your driver is doing anything you believe to be unsafe.
6. Notify your Supervisor of any unsafe drivers or unsafe driving or traveling practices.

CHAPTER 9

Getting Started As a Merchandiser

In This Chapter

❖ Forums and Job Boards
❖ Apply to Merchandising Companies
❖ Visit Local Retailers
❖ Databases
❖ Newspaper Classifieds
❖ Telephone

There are several ways that you can get your foot in the door with any merchandising company, and land a job. Is there work in your area? Probably! There is a demand for your services even if you live in a rural or remote area.

When I started merchandising, I lived in a very rural area. I had all the work I wanted to have. I did have to travel for that work, but I was compensated for it. When I started, my supervisor was from the largest metropolitan area in the state. When she had to travel to my area, she would drive fifty-five minutes and forty-three miles out of the way just to dodge some of our mountain roads. Now my county has become more civilized. We have four-lane roads covering most of the county.

Are there still plenty of jobs available? A resounding yes! I have been off work for three months due to surgery, and I am getting two to three calls a week from merchandising companies I have never heard of, asking me to work.

Wal-Mart, Home Depot, Target, Sears, Costco, Safeway, JC Penney, Kmart, Walgreen, Lowe's, CVS, Best Buy, Publix, Rite Aid, Federated

Department Stores, Gap, Winn-Dixie, Meijer, TJX, Staples, Office Depot, Toys "R" Us, Circuit City, SuperValu Retail, Kohl's, Dillards, OfficeMax, QVC, etc.—are any of these stores within driving distance of you? These are just a few of the top one hundred stores that you may be able to find work in. You may work directly for product manufacturers or retailers, but the vast majorities of these large companies seek the services of and contract with a specialized merchandising company. These companies who contract to perform merchandising services are the ones who directly hire the merchandisers.

When you have no experience, you will usually be taking jobs offered as an Independent Contractor. These were typically one-time projects and an excellent way to gain work experience, but now most companies hire that way unless they expect you to earn more than $600 during the calendar year. With experience on your résumé, you will have a better chance at securing ongoing work as an employee. If there is considerable distance involved, consider accepting work that is en route for you. (As I explained in an earlier chapter.) You can work your way through several different towns, and with mileage compensation, you might find it is worth your time. This is a business decision you will have to make for your particular circumstances.

Forums and Job Boards

Watch Forums and Job Boards to pick up merchandising work. Please note: It is extremely dangerous to post your personal information on forums, such as your home address, home phone, etc. It is best to apply for open jobs via e-mail or as the poster has requested.

Most Merchandising and Mystery Shopping Companies are very reputable, but you can always run into an employee every now and then that is not. I, myself, have my own Employer Identification Number (EIN). An EIN is also known as a Federal Tax Identification Number and is used to identify a business entity. This way I do not have to give anyone my social security number. (I have been the victim of identity theft in the past.)

Apply to Merchandising Companies

Apply to as many merchandising companies as possible. You can apply to any merchandising company regardless of where they are physically located. Their clients and stores are nationwide. Contact companies that have job openings in your state even if the posted job is not in your town. Just ask them to add your name to their database. Use a saved cover letter, and then just e-mail a copy to them. Merchandising Company Listings are included in Appendix 2: Resources.

It is also a good idea to keep track of all the applications and companies to which you have applied. The NCPMS Application Sheet and Company Tracker Sheet helps you track this valuable information. Find both the Application Sheet and Company Tracker in Appendix 3: Business Forms.

Visit Local Retailers

Try going to any mass-merchant stores in your area such as Wal-Mart, Target, and major grocery chains such as Safeway, Albertson's, Winn-Dixie, etc. Ask the claims or receiving clerk, department managers (especially electronics or cosmetic), or store manager if they know of any merchandising companies with openings in their store. The store employees are usually helpful and know if their stores are missing a merchandiser.

Ask to see the store's vendors' log and look for the companies that work in that store. They may currently have a merchandiser, but things can quickly change. They may need a merchandiser immediately, and if you have already contacted them and let them know you are ready, willing, and able to work for them, you may be given first shot at the job.

This next idea came from a forum then run by Cathy Plumb and would require some legwork on your part. Visit your local mass retail or grocery chain and find out the bread, beverage, or snack food delivery schedule. Many companies—such as Pepsi, Coke, Nabisco, Keebler, Frito-Lay, and local bread companies in your area—deliver products to the store by truck. Between deliveries, they hire merchandisers to restock the products on the shelf. Be aware, this will probably involve some weekend work. The truck drivers can give you the office number for those who hire these merchandisers. They are also usually aware if there is an opening in your area and can give you some ideas on what the company requirements are.

Databases

Getting listed in merchandising databases is a great way to get leads delivered straight to your door. You will be contacted when work becomes available in your area.

I personally never pay to be listed in databases, but it could be worth your money if you prefer to set aside some time searching for jobs. But if you have the time, then you can find all the work you want by doing the legwork yourself.

Newspaper Classifieds

Watch your newspaper. Sometimes the merchandising companies place ads. Many regional newspapers now carry their employment classifieds online. Find your hometown newspaper online at News Online, *http:// www.newspapers.com/usacity.htm*.

Telephone

The telephone is a powerful and critical tool in a successful job search. The telephone can get you behind closed doors and will help you contact those hard-to-reach people. It is not wise to call someone and just start talking. Telephone communications in a job search are business calls, not personal calls. Actually, they are sales calls. A business or sales caller has about twenty seconds to capture the attention of the person on the other line. Therefore, communication has to be to the point and concise.

A planned phone call should include the following:

1. Introduction. Tell the person who you are.
2. Lead statement. A quick statement designed to get the person's attention.

3. Body. State your purpose for the call.
4. Close. Accomplish your goal, ask for information, schedule an interview, etc.

Depending on your personal communication skills, you may not feel comfortable using the phone. But give it a try anyway. Remember, the person you are contacting probably started out with a call to the company just like you are doing.

If you want to be viewed as a professional, always respond to job postings with your résumé and cover letter. Recruiters often lament about a contact that says, "Hi, I am interested in the job offer. I can work for you." Then they include no other information like where they live or how they can be contacted.

Just apply, apply, apply . . . and don't get discouraged. It just takes a bit of time to get your name out and then the offers start rolling in. Soon you will be able to "pick and choose."

JUDITH ADKINS-SPEARS

CHAPTER 10

Put Your Best Foot Forward

In This Chapter

- ❖ Résumés
- ❖ Which Type Is Right for You?
- ❖ Seven Tips to Résumé Success
- ❖ Most Common Résumé Goofs
- ❖ Cover Letter
- ❖ Common Errors in Cover Letters
- ❖ Basics for Your Interview
- ❖ Business Cards
- ❖ Thank-You Letter

A successful job search is to successfully market a product—*you*! You need to set yourself apart from the rest to get that job. There are several strategies that can improve your chances of landing a merchandising job, even with little or no experience. Let's look at the different ways to market yourself in the best light possible to find or increase your work as a merchandiser.

Résumés

Your résumé is a Marketing Tool and is usually the first impression an employer will have of you. It needs to market your relevant skills, knowledge, and accomplishments.

Employers usually only spend thirty seconds or so reviewing each résumé; therefore, that first impression needs to be the one that counts. Make sure it presents you in a positive way. It is not enough to have the employment skills that an employer desires if you do not market them.

When applying for a job with an employment application, you may want to attach your résumé. If you are given an application, never write "See résumé." Take the time to fill out the application completely, as the application is part of the preemployment process and omitting it is an act of not following directions. The résumé will add impact and should complement the application.

Which Type of Résumé Is Right for You?

There are three basic résumé formats: Chronological, Functional, and Combined. Determine which format and variation will best display your strengths.

There are four essential elements of a résumé:

- Your name and address
- Personal Objective
- Work History
- Education

Offering personal references is not essential, but it is a good idea to either list the names and addresses of two or three people or to have that information available if a prospective employer asks for references.

Your Name and Address

Be sure to include your full name (no nicknames) and current address. Use the complete street name, including the word Avenue, Road, Street, etc. Make sure that you include your zip code.

Your name and address need to appear on the first page of your résumé. If your résumé is two pages, then be sure that at least your name is on the second page. (Résumés that are longer than two pages might not get processed! Remember that a prospective employer is likely to be reviewing quite a few résumés, so keep your information to the point, and limit yourself to two pages.)

Personal Objective

Include a one-sentence statement that provides your "objective" for applying for the job. This doesn't have to be anything more than your honest reason for looking for work. Try to use your own words (that is, try to write the sentence yourself rather than copying a statement from an example résumé). Use plain language (you won't necessarily impress an employer by using big words).

Examples of a personal objective:

- I am planning on making a career in retail sales and want to learn more about working in a clothing store. I am very artistic and will enjoy working in a craft store.
- I am certified in welding, and I am looking for a job in a welding shop.
- I want to contribute my skills as (an XYZ) to a successful company.

As you can see, the "personal objective" statement is a simple sentence that tells the employer why you are applying for the job.

Work History

Your work history is a list of your last three jobs, with your most recent job first. If you are currently working, then start with that job. Include the name of the company, address, and phone number. For past employment, list at least the company name, city, and state (phone numbers are a plus even if out of state).

Show, in a short list, your primary job duties (tasks) at each job. You don't need to go into a lot of detail. **List only the primary tasks for your job position.** Don't list job duties that don't pertain to your primary job unless it is a skill that is applicable to the job you are applying for.

Do this for your two prior jobs. If you've only had one job, then obviously, only list that job.

Education

For most folks, this is going to be relatively simple. List college education (college name, degree earned, and year degree was awarded) and then high school (high school name and year graduated).

If you only have some college credits, then only list those pertinent for the job you are applying for. That is, don't list World History 101 if you are applying for a job as a cashier. However, if you have taken Principles of Management, and you are applying for a job as a shift leader or floor supervisor, then this is education that pertains to the job.

For people who have earned a GED or other vocational certificates, list those. Provide the educational facility that you attended and the year you received the GED or certificate.

If you have copies of degrees, certificates, or other educational awards, then take them with you to the interview. Do not attach them to your résumé unless the job application specifically requests them. However, be sure to take copies with you for your job interview, and offer them to the interviewer.

There is no need to provide addresses or phone numbers of the schools. However, if you have this information, be sure to take it with you to the interview.

References (Optional)

References are people who may be contacted by a prospective employer and asked to provide work-related or personal information about you. Be sure to verify that your references are willing to be contacted and will be comfortable in answering a few questions about you. Use each person's full name and current telephone number (even if out of state).

If you have written references (from prior employers, teachers, or friends), be sure to take copies with you to the job interview. That way, you can offer your interviewer a copy that can be kept with your job application (and you won't inconvenience the interviewer by having to make a copy of an original during the interview).

Which Résumé Format Is Right for You?

Many job seekers agonize over which résumé format to use—chronological or functional? Will choosing one format over the other impact the effectiveness of the résumé? Yes, it can, but not in the way that most job seekers think it will.

Not all job candidates will want to chronicle everything they have done. Age discrimination isn't always actually about age. It's about all the things that are erroneously assumed to go along with being older, such as being out of touch, less technologically aware, etc.

The résumé is a chance for you to show you're not any of those things. Here are some tips:

- Trim some early experiences, such as jobs older than ten to fifteen years.
- Include links to social networking profiles, such as LinkedIn, Facebook, Twitter, or Plaxo. Set up such profiles to be highly professional, not personal.
- Add information about hobbies if they are sports related.
- Consider removing graduation dates.

Show that you are an invigorated job candidate who's not even close to peaking in your career. Illustrate that you've been keeping your skills refreshed, such as through certification courses, ongoing study, volunteer work, and membership in professional organizations.

The two types of résumé formats are very different. Chronological format details the job history in reverse time order, starting with the most recent position and working backward. This format is the one that most recruiters and hiring managers prefer.

Chronological Format

Benefits to using a chronological résumé include:

- Shows your results. The reader can specifically see when and where a candidate achieved results. The guesswork is eliminated.

- Shows your range. A chronological format highlights flexibility. Many job seekers have held varying positions over their careers, often in different functions and roles. A good strategy is to showcase that diversity.
- Shows your record of success. The progression of a candidate's career, records of promotion, and increases in responsibility are shown clearly. These attest to a candidate's performance record and drive to succeed.

Some job seekers worry about employment. Small gaps in employment (a year or less) are common these days. Layoffs and mergers impact nearly everyone's lives. Handled strategically, they can be minimized in a chronological résumé.

Functional Format

Also known as a "skills résumé" it has the content arranged according to performance type and function. A human resource professional for example, might divide his/her skills into categories such as Employee Training, Benefits Management, and Workforce Development. Under each category, the relevant information would be listed or described.

A brief work history listing comes at the end of the document listing job title, employer, and dates. I've seen some functional résumés with no employment dates at all.

A functional format is generally chosen when attempting to make a career change or to minimize a career blemish. Often, the functional format is used when a large span of time is missing from the work history.

Most people hold jobs for eighteen months to five years, and gaps in between are not unusual. Life happens to everyone. Layoffs occur, parents get sick, and people decide to go back to college for an advanced degree. A gap in between jobs of any length used to be a deadly problem but it is fairly common across everyone's career paths these days. There are some ways to handle date gaps on résumés, so you as the job seeker shouldn't feel there is a big flashing neon sign there that says "Unemployed"!

JUDITH ADKINS-SPEARS

Years, Not Months

The simplest way to make date gaps "disappear" on a résumé is to not include the months of employment on the job chronology but rather just use years. For example, Dave was laid off in February of 2008 from XYZ Company and spent four months job searching before signing on with a new company, ABC Inc., in June of the same year. He is now looking to make a voluntary move to a different company where he will have more growth potential. That four-month date gap back in 2008 will not show if he notates his jobs with years of employment only.

Ignore It

Yes, ignore it. If the date gap was six months or less or if it doesn't show when the résumé is organized in terms of years of employment, then why bring it up? Fairly short date gaps are not that unusual. A job search can often take weeks or even months to complete. If it doesn't show on the résumé, then don't worry about it.

Address It

Let's say you've been out of work for a longer stretch of time in order to care for an ailing parent (or some other reason). Address that directly in the résumé. Explain the time span. If you were on leave of absence or maybe you were just taking a sabbatical, then give information. A large gap is better explained in some way rather than ignored completely. The explanation given should not be elaborate or detailed. Keep it simple. If the reader wants more information about it, then it can be brought up in the interview.

Problems associated with the functional résumé:

- Where's the information? Recruiters and hiring managers dislike hunting for information. They want to see past performance, and they want to understand your background.
- What's the context? The functional format takes away all frames of reference. A candidate might claim attaining a record-breaking sales contract, but the reader is unable to place that in context in terms of

time and employer. Was that success in sales recent or ten years ago? It's difficult to tell in a functional résumé.

- What's the problem? Recruiters and hiring managers know that the functional format is often used to try to cover something up. The functional format serves as a red flag—"What is this candidate trying to hide?" The use of the format to overcome a detriment actually serves to draw attention to it.

Combination Format

The combination résumé brings the best of both the chronological and functional résumés. It features a functional section that highlights skills, experience, and accomplishments. It also includes a chronological listing of employment, education, and employment-related experiences. The combination résumé is a very effective format for many job seekers. The best chronological résumé can be enhanced with a section highlighting skills, accomplishments, and experience. The functional résumé can be strengthened with a chronological listing of employment experiences.

Today's job seeker is wise to stick with the chronological format as it provides the necessary information to urge the reader to contact the candidate for an interview.

Seven Tips to Résumé Success

1. Select the best format. While most résumés are written in a historical chronological format, often a better technique is to evenly balance between skill set description, achievements, and employment.
2. Find a balance between wordiness and lack of detail. Employers need to see details about your work history and experience, but they don't need to know everything. Keep information germane to the goal of attaining an interview. Eliminate information that is not related and will not have direct impact on winning the interview.
3. Do not use personal pronouns. "I," "me," "my," "mine," and "our" should not be on a résumé. Résumés are written in first person (implied). Example: For your prior job description, instead of writing "I hired, trained, and supervised a team of assistant managers and sales associates,"

you would instead state that you "hired, trained, and supervised a team of assistant managers and sales associates." Fragment sentences are perfectly acceptable on a résumé and are actually preferred.

4. Use numerical symbols for numbers. While we are taught in school to spell out numbers less than ten, in résumé writing, numerical symbols serve as "eye stops" and are a much-better method. Instead of writing "developed a dynamic team of eight consultants," it would be much more advantageous to state, "Developed a dynamic team of 8 consultants."

5. Think *accomplishments* rather than *job duties*. What makes you stand out from the crowd? How did you come up with a way to do things better, more efficiently, or for less cost? What won honors for you? Information such as this is vital, will gain attention, and will put your résumé to the top of the list.

6. Keep it positive. Reason for leaving a job and setbacks do not have a place on a résumé. Employers are seeking people who can contribute and have successfully performed in the past. Concentrate on communicating these issues and avoid any detracting information.

7. Be phone savvy. Many first-time job interviews are conducted via telephone rather than in person. Make sure you are prepared for that telephone call when it arrives . . . and make sure you have a résumé that will make the phone ring!

Résumés should be sent to a person by name. Avoid sending the résumé to a job title such as Human Resource Manager. It will take extra effort, but do your research and find out the name and title of the appropriate person to whom your résumé should be sent. Send your résumé to the employer even if they are not hiring. You never know what the future will bring.

Most Common Résumé Goofs

E-mail Errors

One of the most common goofs we see is an incorrect e-mail address. Since most job search efforts are centered around e-mail communications, having an e-mail address that is wrong or difficult to interpret can be a pothole in your road to success. Double-check your e-mail address to make sure it is correct. Don't use your work e-mail address on your résumé and try to avoid using the number one when making an email address because it is difficult to tell if it is a letter or a numeral. Avoid goofy or cutesy e-mail monikers such as vanhalenlvr83 or similar. E-mail systems that use automated spam authenticators are loathed by recruiters and line managers alike, so stay away from them during your job search. Remember, you can set up an e-mail address that you *use just* for job search.

Mechanical Mistakes

Misspellings are the most common mechanical mistake. People rely on spell-check too much. Spell-check can't tell the difference, though, in meaning. If you write "manger" instead of "manager," then spell-check won't flag it. Other mechanical problems include verb-tense shift and capitalization. It seems like, when in doubt, job seekers will capitalize something just "to be on the safe side," but that just creates an error.

Fluff Phrases

The profile or summary is often the most difficult section of the résumé to create. As a result, job seekers fall back on soft-skill phrases or fluff phrases such as "good communicator" or "hardworking." These sound good, but they tell the reader nothing. These are subjective traits that are opinion-based. You may think you are a good communicator, but your peers might say otherwise. These traits will be judged in the interview, so don't load the résumé down with these. Remember, 99.9 percent of all the other candidates will also be claiming these skills. Have you ever heard of anyone putting "bad communicator" or "lazy with sloppy attention to detail" on the résumé?

Too Much Information (TMI)

Job seekers often forget for whom they are writing. The recruiter or hiring manager is going to be skim-reading the résumé and will be looking for the main points. The job seeker, on the other hand, feels it's necessary to put every bit of information possible in the résumé, right down to including that Eagle Scout designation from 1984. Having too much information, or irrelevant information, is a common résumé error.

Too Little Information (TLI)

The opposite of TMI is TLI—too little information. Being too general in the résumé is just as bad as being too wordy. Usually too little information takes the form of no details on achievements. Most people can get their job duties or role descriptions down but falter when it's time to detail their successes in some sort of quantitative or qualitative way. As a result, the content is thin or bland and doesn't inspire the reader to make contact with the job seeker.

Passive Voice

We are all taught that formal writing is passive voice writing. Most people have a tendency to write in the passive voice, especially when composing their résumés. Passive voice—"responsible for," "duties included," etc.—is weak writing. Résumés need to be powerful sales documents, and passive voice doesn't persuade the reader. Make sure the résumé is written in active voice with lots of solid keywords throughout the content.

Personal Information

The fact that you are an avid skeeball player, or that you collect old-world coins, has no relevance to whether or not you are qualified for the position. So why include information on hobbies, sports, or interests?

Poor Design

The old large left-margin layout is out-of-fashion. Fancy long designs, images, or tables will really give the databases a hard time when you upload your résumé. The best thing to do when it comes to design of your résumé is KISS—keep it simple, sweetie. Yes, make it appealing, but overdesigned résumés will get scrambled in uploads, and thus will not win interviews.

One-Page Length

One-page résumés are long gone unless you are a new graduate without much experience. Having said that, we still see plenty of one-page résumés for more senior job seekers. It does not surprise me! When a job seeker tries to limit the content of the résumé to fit into one page, he/she is cutting vital information to adhere to a "rule" that is not valid for most résumés. Many résumés (including midlevel) are two pages in length, and three pages are acceptable for some senior-level candidates.

Cover Letter

The cover letter, which is a one-page letter of self-introduction, is also just as easy to prepare. The letter should be brief, no more than three paragraphs of two or three sentences each, and should state your intention for applying for the job and reasons that you are a good candidate for that job.

For both the résumé and the cover letter, never try to sound like anyone other than *you*. Remember, you are the person who will be in the interview. You will be talking. You will be answering questions. If you have your sister-in-law or your next-door neighbor, write your cover letter and résumé in his or her own language, then the interviewer will be expecting to talk to an applicant who speaks the same way. If you need help, then, of course, ask for help, but write the résumé and the cover letter yourself.

Common Errors in Cover Letters

Not Addressed to a Specific Person

"To Whom It May Concern" is a poor start for a cover letter. Do some research and find out the name of the person to whom the package should be directed. If you absolutely cannot find to whom it should go, then aim high. If you send it to the head of the company or the head of the department, then it will have a better chance of getting to the decision maker than if you simply send it to the HR department.

It can be difficult to know how to start a cover letter when the résumé / cover letter is submitted online, and there is no name (and sometimes not even a company name). An alternative to a greeting is to indicate the job-posting number or title, and perhaps where the job was posted in a reference line at the beginning of the cover letter; for example: "RE: Marketing Assistant Position—ID number 3456"

Wrong Audience

Depending on the type of recipient, the cover letter will vary in content and approach. A cover letter to a network contact will be somewhat different in content and tone than a cover letter to a blind job contact, for the same information normally not included in a cover letter goes directly to the employer, such as information about salary, availability, and relocation. A broadcast cover letter will be set up differently than a cover letter going directly to a specific person. Make sure you are aware of the differences, and use the right approach for the audience.

"I" Focused

It is much too easy to start every sentence in a cover letter with "I" or "My," so don't fall to the temptation. Repetitively saying "I" turns off the reader. Vary your sentence structure and focus on your achievements and results. It makes for better communication all around.

Too Long / Too Short

A cover letter should not run past one page. If you have more than that, then you know you are being wordy. Three to four paragraphs is a general rule of thumb. If you will be e-mailing your cover letter in the body of the e-mail with your résumé attached, then be briefer than if you were sending it in a more traditional manner or as an attached document. People are accustomed to short, to-the-point e-mail messages, so don't go overboard with detail.

Irrelevant Information

Sometimes people seem to think they can include information in the cover letter that certainly has no place in the résumé. A good example would be a reason for leaving an employer. Reason for leaving is irrelevant—focus on the future and how you can make a contribution to a new employer. Health status is another issue that sometimes shows up in a cover letter—"I am in good health, energetic, and ready to get started." Anything that reveals age, religion, ethnicity, etc., should be withheld from both the cover letter and résumé. Employers are very wary of litigation and fair hiring practices. Including information that is not needed/wanted by an employer will hurt, not help.

Poor Appearance

Your cover letter should have a name header at the top that matches the header on your résumé—like a letterhead. Make sure your font size is large enough to be easily read. Keep the alignment of your margins clean and even. The balance from the top of the page to the bottom should be appropriate; avoid large white voids above or below the text by balancing the text visually.

Not Signed

When sending by e-mail, make sure you use a businesslike signature without personal mottos and slogans. "Save the endangered snail darter" might be part of your e-mail signature to friends and family, but it has no place on an e-mailed cover letter. Create a signature for job search that contains your contact information, such as phone numbers and e-mail address. A branding line might also be appropriate, for example, "Joe Smith, Software Developer."

You wouldn't wear just one shoe to a job interview, so don't send your résumé without an accompanying cover letter. Be professional, but speak to the reader in an appropriate manner. Use the cover letter to highlight your best value and experience. Point out what makes you unique out of the hundreds of other applicants and grab the attention of the reader. Just like the résumé, make sure you have *no* typos. And of course, avoid these deadly cover-letter errors!

Being ever the one to poke fun at myself, I am inserting a copy of an old cover letter I once sent to a prospective employer. I got the greeting and closing correct, so I'll just include the body. No wonder I didn't get the job! Just look at all these glaring errors!

In addition to this cover letter, I included my Education from first grade through Graduate School and my Employment from 1968 through the present time. At least one plus on my side is that I did send a thank-you letter.

> _____ *has told me there may, in the near future, be an opening for a District Manager in our new company, so I am enclosing a resume. In this note I want to explain a couple of things that just didn't seem to fit in the resume.*

I am 57 yoa. I have been married to the same man since 1968. We have two children, one boy and one girl. Each has one daughter. My daughter has a son due in August. My husband is also a retired teacher. He sells life insurance and coaches' girls' high school basketball. As you can see we have a pretty full life, but both children live in Florida so we have no children or grandchildren around to occupy any time or energy.

I am the oldest girl in a family of six children. My mother was a teacher and my father was the principal of what at the time was the largest school in _____ County. I grew up in the country, on a farm. We raised our own food: cows for milk, chickens for eggs, pigs for you know what, and so forth.

_____ often talks about the little extra effort I put in, but to me that's not extra, that's doing what it takes to do the job properly. If my mother had ever walked into a store behind me I would have wanted to be proud of how it looked. She always said, "If a job's worth doing, it's worth doing right."

It's true I have not supervised large groups of people, but who had when they first started? What I didn't list on my resume, because it's not something I'm proud of, but for one l-o-n-g year I owned and operated a redneck bar. It's a long story how I got roped into it, but by the time my one year's lease was up I had sold the bar. Anyway, I did supervise five employees and at times over 100 drunk, redneck, hillbillies. And that's a mean feat for anyone, at anytime!

I also supervised roomfuls of students ranging in age from twelve to fifty. I was in charge of the entire middle school for weeks at a time when the principal was away.

I know Kentucky, West Virginia, and Eastern Virginia very well. I have traveled these roads doing mystery shopping/merchandising. I am used to traveling alone and for long periods of time. It does not bother me to go into a new territory or to meet new people.

I feel I have a lot to contribute to _____, and not just as a vendor. I prepare myself for each job as I did when I was in college or doing lesson plans to teach a class. When I was a MSN technician I had a different manual prepared for each type of software. I don't expect everyone to be that thorough, but they should know where to find the answers should they ever need them.

Thank you for your time.

The Interview

Telephone Interview

The telephone is a powerful tool in marketing your qualifications to an employer. It is almost guaranteed that you will talk to a potential employer on the telephone at some point in the hiring process.

The purpose of an interview is to get acquainted and to learn about one another. Employers evaluate your qualifications for the job. You help them with this evaluation by being prepared to sell your skills and experience.

It is also an opportunity for you to evaluate the employer. Since these interviews will often occur unexpectedly, have any key information, including your résumé, next to the phone. You will sound prepared if you don't have to search for information. Keep your résumé in view and refer to it as needed. Focus on skills, experiences, and accomplishments.

Make sure you also have a notepad and pen so you can jot down notes and any questions you would like to ask at the end of the interview. Be prepared to think on your feet: If you are asked to participate in a role-playing situation, then give short but concise answers. Accept any criticism with tact and grace.

If you are offered a job, then be prepared to negotiate hourly wage / project fee and mileage. Know in advance how much you are willing to accept for compensation and mileage. Be prepared with distances of your work areas. If they hesitate to pay additional, then remind them of your experience or skills. If you are not experienced, then consider accepting the job anyway. You will then have experience and a negotiating point the next time you are offered work. However, you must take care to neither take advantage of the situation nor underestimate your opportunities.

Additional Telephone Tips

1. Wear a smile on the telephone—they may not see it, but they will hear it.
2. If you have not previously sent a résumé to the potential employer, then always take the initiative to offer to send it to them.
3. If you have already sent a résumé to a potential employer, then a follow-up phone call to check on your résumé might turn into a telephone interview.
4. After ending the interaction, evaluate your phone call. What went well in the call? How can you improve?

Basics for Your In-Person Interview

Attire

No matter what the working environment of the company, dress conservatively. Men should wear a suit and tie, women should wear a suit. Stick with conservative colors—dark blue, black, or gray. Think "business—professional."

Make sure all the details are covered. You want to go into the interview looking impeccable. Don't give them a reason to prejudge you. Review the checklist below:.

- Clean and press interview suit. Make sure it looks sharp.
- Polish your shoes.
- Get a haircut if you need one. You want to look your best.
- Make sure any facial hair is trimmed neatly.
- Cut your nails. Many people forget this.
- Wear little or no jewelry.

Timeliness

Be on time. Find out what your itinerary is. If you are unsure of the company location, give yourself some extra time to get there. If you are going to be late for any reason, then call the company and let them know immediately. If you need to reschedule the interview, then contact your recruiter immediately. Review and don't forget to bring the following.

- Directions to the company
- Main phone number for company
- Name of the interviewer
- Phone number/extension of the interviewer
- Phone number and/or pager of your recruiter

Items to Bring

Be prepared with any documentation that you may need. You might have to fill out an application requiring accurate past employment dates. Review and don't forget to bring the following.

- Several copies of your résumé (one for each interviewer)
- Letters of commendation/recommendation
- Past reviews from previous/current employers
- Pad of paper and a pen
- A small planner or professional binder to hold documents, paper, pen, etc.
- List of your own questions that you want to ask (covered later)

Warming Up

Make sure you shake the hand of each person you are introduced to. It is important to remember the names as you are introduced. Repeating the name as you greet the person is a good technique for memory recall. For example, "Nice to meet you, *Rick.*"

Oftentimes, the interview starts with an ice-breaking question, such as, "Tell me about yourself, Judy."

Spend two to three minutes discussing your background, education, experiences, etc. Be brief and do not go off on a tangent. Try to tie the end of your monologue into your current situation. You want to take this opportunity to let them know that you have researched their company and you choose them (i.e., "so I learned this new technology and your company works in that very area so that's why I am here today.")

Speak to their needs

The majority of the interview is going to be about three things:

- What you have done in your past to qualify you for the job.
- Why you are looking for a new opportunity.
- What you can do for the company.

It is paramount to answer each question in terms of what they are looking for. Be specific and don't be afraid to ask questions. Remember the Magic Formula (*stop, think, ask*) if the interviewer asks you, "Why do you believe you can do the job?"

STOP, THINK, ASK

"From your prospective [*interviewer's name*], what do you require for a [*position title*] to do?

Remember, use the person's name often. It builds a sense of familiarity. See *How to Win Friends and Influence People* by Dale Carnagie

Then answer specifically to the wants and needs of the question.

As you can see from this example, ask what they need. Speak to their needs. Expand on your background to support how you have overcome similar obstacles. And remember to be specific!

Do Your Homework

Answering to the needs of the interviewers require that you do your homework before the interview.Make sure you know the following about the company.

- History
- Products
- Competitors
- Website
- Interviewer(s) background if possible

Questions to Ask

People sometimes forget that a job interview is a two-sided process. You should be prepared with a list of questions to ask. Here are some good examples.

- Type of company, etc.
- Type of employer/interviewer
- Who else will I be interacting with?
- Why is this position open?
- What happened to the last person doing this job?
- What is the number one priority in this position? Expand on that point.
- Projects—past, present, and future.
- What are first year's goals in this position?
- What obstacles do you see that could stop you from meeting these goals?

You might also want to have a list of your goals and have it in writing. This would not be for anyone but yourself, but it is good to have it written down because you will be asked about your goals.

Salary Questions

If it can be avoided, do not discuss salary unless the interviewer(s) brings it up. If you are asked about salary, a good response is as follows:

> "Currently, my salary is [—amount]. I would expect my next salary to be a fair offer for someone with my level of experience."

This is a nice way to sidestep the salary question, if it comes up.

Close for the Job

At the end of each part of the interview (with each person), you have an important question to ask. This is the most important question in the interview process. Time and again, people don't ask this question, and they end up not getting the job because of it. The question is,

"Do I have the qualifications you are looking for?"

If they say *yes*, then ask, "What is the next step?"

If they say *no* or "Not Sure," then you must find out why by asking, "I must not have covered something, what concerns do you have?"

This gives you a chance to answer any concerns immediately and avoid coming back for another interview. Please remember that this is the most important question that you will ask in the interview!

Business Cards

Get yourself some professional Business Cards. Order free customizable business cards at Vistaprint.com, and you will find them useful. They cost about $5 for S/H, but they will pay for themselves many times over. Send one with each résumé you submit by mail. When you meet other merchandisers in the field, give them a card for future job opportunities. They are also handy to leave on bulletin boards/walls where vendors sign in at stores. When supervisors come in to do work in open areas, there is your card.

Thank-You Letter

Always send a thank-you letter. Make sure you have the names and correct spellings of each person you interview with. In the letter, make sure three things are covered.

- Thank them for their time.
- Reiterate that you have the skills they are looking for and that you can do the job.
- Tell them you want the job.

CHAPTER 11

Taking Care of Your New Business

In This Chapter

❖ Hobby or Business?
❖ Successful Merchandisers Pay Taxes
❖ Twenty-One Merchandising Business Tax Deductions
❖ Setting up your Home Office
❖ Merchandising Companies
❖ Record Keeping

Important Note: Tax advice from a professional is always a good idea, but with a home business, it's more than a good idea. It's essential. Please consult with a tax advisor on all issues discussed below, and any other questions you may have before you file your tax documents. The advice below is just advice, check with a professional for the last word on these issues. The cost of their advice will be paid back to you many times over in savings and peace of mind!

First, keep in mind that it is your option whether to treat your merchandising activities as a business or not. This section will be especially relevant for merchandisers who choose to treat their merchandising as a business and reap the rewards the IRS offers for small businesses. Obviously, it takes more work to treat merchandising this way. For most people, though, the extra work involved means many hundreds or even thousands back come tax time!

It is important to remember that while you are eligible for many great tax write-offs by being self-employed, the income you earn as a merchandiser is taxable income, and you are responsible for declaring all of it.

As you read on, you may be surprised at the number of deductions you can take for legitimate business expenses that you never knew were expenses.

However, if you really do begin to make good money with merchandising, you'll want to get all the deductions you're eligible for under law. It's just good common sense: don't pay more in taxes than you're obligated to.

Perhaps one of the first things you should understand is that when a merchandising company pays you, you are responsible for declaring this income even if they don't send you a 1099 form at the end of the year. If a single employer pays you more than $600 in a year, then they are responsible for sending you a 1099. Whether they do or do not, you, as a merchandiser, are still responsible for paying taxes on the income.

I have heard merchandisers say, "If the companies don't send me a 1099, then I'm not going to file. They didn't send anything to the IRS, so who will know?" Nobody may know right now. But suppose the company is audited? Then the IRS has everyone that company paid even $1 to during that year. Now you're going to say, "I suppose you think the IRS is going to go after little ole me, who made $40 from Company XYZ?" Maybe, maybe not. I, myself, am not going to take that chance. Are you?

Hobby or Business?

The IRS states that, "generally, an activity qualifies as a business if it is carried on with the reasonable expectation of earning a profit."

In order to make this determination, taxpayers should consider the following factors:

- Does the time and effort put into the activity indicate an intention to make a profit?
- Does the taxpayer depend on income from the activity?
- If there are losses, then are they due to circumstances beyond the taxpayer's control, or did they occur in the start-up phase of the business?
- Has the taxpayer changed methods of operation to improve profitability?
- Does the taxpayer have the knowledge needed to carry on the activity as a successful business?
- Has the taxpayer made a profit in similar activities in the past?

- Does the activity make a profit in some years?

The IRS presumes that an activity is carried on for profit if it makes a profit during at least three of the last five tax years, including the current year. If an activity is not for profit, then losses from that activity may not be used to offset other income. An activity produces a loss when related expenses exceed income.

In general, taxpayers may deduct ordinary and necessary expenses for conducting a trade or business.

An ordinary expense is an expense that is common and accepted in the merchandising business. A necessary expense is one that is helpful and appropriate for the profession. This is important because an expense does not have to be indispensable to be considered necessary. For more specifics, consult your tax advisor and review the IRS's Schedule C 2011 Instructions.

Successful Merchandisers Pay Taxes

As a merchandiser and independent contractor, you are paid cash with no taxes deducted. You are therefore responsible for paying city, state, and federal income tax just like a business, and you are responsible for paying it directly to the government.

Federal and state income taxes must be paid in estimated quarterly payments (check for any city rules). These payments are due in four installments on: April 15, June 15, September 15, and January 15. The federal taxes also cover your "self-employment tax" which includes a payment for social security and Medicare.

Being responsible for these taxes yourself is expensive because when you were a regular employee, your company paid for half your Medicare and social security tax. Now, you're responsible for all of it though a portion of it is deductible.

Generally, you are obligated to pay estimated quarterly tax if you think you'll owe at least $500 in tax that year. In addition, you'll need to estimate accurately, as there are penalties if you severely underestimate.

If you don't make your tax payments on schedule and according to the rules, then you could be liable for penalties plus interest on the money you owe.

Your tax preparer should provide you with forms and envelopes for making your estimated payments, or you can order these forms directly from the IRS by calling 800-829-3676.

Twenty-One Merchandising Business Tax Deductions

So now, you know that you'll owe taxes if you're at all successful in merchandising. The key is offsetting some of this success, so your tax burden is not so high. Fortunately, the government provides many generous write-offs for the self-employed businessperson.

Every time you buy a ream of paper, pay an insurance premium, or travel to a merchandising job, you're incurring a legitimate business expense that may be tax-deductible. If you keep good records of these expenses, by the end of the year, you could have a sizeable amount to help lessen your payment or even get you a refund.

Here are some of the most common deductions taken by home businesses and merchandisers. Take these ideas to your tax professional, and discuss them with him/her for an "action plan" on these and other techniques so you can save money through smart merchandising expense planning.

1. Internet and e-mail services are deductible

    Since so much of what you do in merchandising revolves around the Internet, and since your merchandising companies deliver you jobs though the Internet, you can deduct your monthly bill for your online service providers such as DSL or dial-up.

2. First-year equipment expense deduction

    Using the first-year expense deduction, you can deduct up to $133,000 worth of business equipment—computers, fax machines, copiers, phone systems, or other fixed assets. Otherwise, you'd have to deduct the cost of the equipment over several years using the IRS's depreciation schedules.

3. Rent (Mortgage), phones, utilities

A portion of your rent (mortgage); your electricity, water or gas bills; and your home and cell phone charges are all deductible. (It will be discussed later in this chapter how to compute these deductions.)

4. Auto expenses

If you use your car to drive to merchandising jobs, you can choose from two methods to deduct your business use of the car. The most-used method is to deduct the amount per mile that the IRS allows for business travel—in 2010, it was 50¢ per mile. On the other hand, you can take a depreciation deduction for the cost of your vehicle and add the costs of running and maintaining the car (expenses like parking, insurance, gas, oil, repairs, toll fees, tires, licensing, and registrations). You are not locked into one method once you start. From year to year, you can switch between methods. Consult your tax advisor on the best method for you.

5. Entertainment

You can deduct 50 percent of business expenses for entertaining a client, customer, or employee if it is directly related to your business or associated with your business. But for this deduction, you must keep excellent records! If you take someone out for a meal, you must record the person, the date, the total amount; the place the meal took place, the business purpose of the meal, and your business relationship.

6. Further Education and Certifications

If you've taken a course or achieved certifications and incurred a fee, then don't neglect to claim these as deductions for education expenses that relate to your merchandising business. The IRS requires education expenses must maintain or improve skills required in your present employment or required by your employers or as a legal requirement of your profession.

7. Health Insurance

   If you're self-employed you can deduct a significant portion of your health insurance payments. You can then add the remainder you can't deduct to your itemized medical expenses. If all these expenses together exceed 7.5 percent of your gross income, then your further medical expenses are 100 percent deductible. Check with your tax advisor for the latest *amounts* and percentages concerning health insurance deductions.

8. Home-office deduction

   If you work out of your home as your principal place of business, then you are eligible for a break on your taxes. This means you cannot work at the kitchen table or in a den that your family uses at night, but you must have a room set aside for use solely as an office. This does not mean, however, that all your business must be performed in the office. This is important for merchandisers. For example, if you're in your office for ten hours a week writing reports, applying for jobs, and managing your business, but you're out on merchandising jobs thirty hours a week, you should still be eligible for the home-office deduction.

   - What can be deducted with the home-office deduction? Home-office deductions include a percentage of your rent or cost of owning your home, based on the square footage your office takes up as a percentage of your home. For example, if you live in a 1,500-square-foot home, and your office takes up 150 square feet, then you can deduct 10 percent of your rent or home cost. You're also eligible to deduct 10 percent of other expenses such as home insurance, utilities, cleaning service, repairs, and maintenance, trash collection, and many more. Check with your tax advisor for specific recommendations.
   - A note of caution on the home deduction. There may be instances where the home-office deduction is not right for you financially. If you are a homeowner and plan to sell your house any time soon, taking the home-office tax deduction over the years may mean that you have some taxes to pay when you sell.

If you take the home-office deduction, you have declared a part of your home as a business property. At the home's sale, the IRS will want you to pay tax on at least some of the depreciation you've taken. For example, if you bought a home for $50,000, sold it for $100,000, and claimed 10 percent of the house as a business deduction, then you have a $50,000 gain that the IRS sees as $45,000 personal and $5,000 business gain. That business gain is immediately taxable. In addition, if you had claimed $10,000 in depreciation for business years over the years, the IRS will want you to pay tax on that as well. Sound confusing? Just consult your tax advisor before taking the home-office deduction.

9. Retirement plans

   As a self-employed business owner, you have a wide variety of retirement plans available to you, including IRAs, Simplified Employee Pensions (SEPs), and Keogh accounts. You can deduct contributions made to these plans, and their income is tax deferred.

10. Trade shows, conventions, and seminars

    The costs of attending a trade show, convention, or seminar can be considered legitimate business expenses.

11. Professional publications

    Magazines, newspapers, newsletters, or books related to merchandising are deductible.

12. Interest payments on business credit cards

    If you have a separate business credit card, then you can deduct interest payments.

13. Professional associations

    You can deduct dues for joining a trade association such as the MSPA, your chamber of commerce, or any other professional group related to

JUDITH ADKINS-SPEARS

merchandising such as ShadowShopper.com. You cannot deduct dues for a private club such as social and athletic clubs.

14. Local travel

In addition to the deductions for your car travel, you can also deduct for expenses related to travel by taxi, train, or bus related to your merchandising business. Keep track of your travels in a datebook, and get receipts.

15. Business travel

If you go overnight for a convention or a merchandising assignment, then you can deduct all expenses related to the trip, including transportation, lodging, meals, laundry expenses, cleaning, fax, or phone charges, tips, etc.

16. Parking

You can deduct garage, lot, and meter charges. But don't try to deduct a ticket for letting the meter run out or running a red light on the way to a merchandising assignment.

17. Postage

Any postage costs you incur as part of your merchandising assignments are deductible. Try to use your business credit card when buying postage, so you have a better record to the purchase.

18. Office furniture

Desks, chairs, lamps, rugs, filing cabinets, couches, plants . . . they're all business expenses.

19. Office supplies

Keep track of money you spend on everything in your office from paper clips to legal pads, and toner cartridges to file folders. Most all office supplies are deductible.

20. Local business taxes and fees

If you have to pay city, county, or state business taxes, or other fees, these charges are deductible on your federal income tax statement.

21. Bank service charges

If your bank is charging you for your business account, then you can write off these costs.

Finally, remember that tax issues are important, and that you should be sure that you investigate everything that you can deduct and cannot deduct by speaking with a tax advisor. Another important resource is the IRS, which has a helpful information pamphlet called IRS Publication 587 "Business Use of Your Home."

Setting up your Home Office

Everyone who does merchandising seriously should have a home office. Organization and Time Management is the framework of a merchandiser's job and reputation. A properly set up home office space can help you stay organize and keep your business running successfully.

Here are the basic items that you will need:

Workspace area

This can be as simple as a space in a spare bedroom but somewhere where you can keep all your merchandising information together.

Storage area

When merchandising, you will receive supplies and materials from the company to use on your next store visit. These all need a safe place to call home until you take them to your store. Also you will need space to keep your merchandisers bag and tools. If you are working for multiple companies, then these can take a little bit of space too.

JUDITH ADKINS-SPEARS

Office supplies

All the basics such as Paper, pencils, pens, stapler, Wite out, Post-it notes, scissors, envelopes, stamps, etc.

Desk

You need a place to keep your office supplies for your business, and you need a place to work on all your paperwork.

File Cabinet

This is a must to keep all your completed paperwork in order. It is also an excellent place to keep company contact info and company policy paperwork.

Calendar

A calendar is essential to keep track of all your projects and when they are due. If you don't use a calendar, then some other sort of system will be necessary like a daily planner or use the Daily Log business form available in the Appendix 3: Business Forms in the back of the book. Don't leave your projects' time frames to memory—you will forget and may possibly lose your job because of it.

Computer with Internet Connection

This is essential in our business now since most companies operate on the Internet. It is one of the best ways to pick up jobs and is increasingly the choice of companies to report your completed projects online. I also like to e-mail my supervisors with questions that are not time sensitive. That gives my supervisor the chance to respond at their convenience.

Printer

Though not essential on your first job, you will find that you need one. Many companies send forms and instructions by e-mail or download them from their website. You will need to be able to print off the necessary paperwork to take with you to your job.

Fax and Copier

It is also helpful to have access to a photocopier and a fax. (Keep in mind that the most economical printers made today are really the printer/copier/fax combo.) Make sure you have the fax number in advance. Many companies will ask if they can fax paperwork to you. E-fax, as mentioned previously, is an option for fax, also.

Second phone line

I highly recommend a second phone line for your computer connection. It would be a terrible thing to be using your only phone line for your computer when a recruiter was trying to call you for work!

You may find additional items helpful in your home office, but these items will get you started.

Merchandising Companies

Keep a list of all companies you have applied with. If you do not hear from them within six months, then reapply. There is no set way to keep up with all the companies you contact. One way I have tried is to keep a "Company" address book. This book has nobody personal in it. It is strictly Business. Listings are in alphabetical order by Company name and by Scheduler name. Schedulers often only give their first name. I'm a little weird in my address books, so I list people by first name and add another listing to list them by their last name if I know it. With the scheduler's name is listed the merchandising company they work with and for whom they in turn schedule. On the company's listing, it has the address, phone number—800 and their local—fax number, website, data site, e-mail address and my company ID and password.

I think I have now found a better, more economical way to maintain these records. I set up a folder for each company I apply to. The form I use is included in Appendix 3: Business Forms. I include Company Name, Website Address, Mailing Address, Contact Person, Phone, Fax, Hours of Operation, Jobsite Webpage, Date Applied, Approved, Username or

Personal ID number, Password, Company Specialty, and any pertinent notes.

Record Keeping

Organize Your Records

Keeping accurate records and proof of expenses is not only to track your profit margin but also for easier tax time and accurate payment verification. If a payment discrepancy is found, then your saved paperwork becomes the proof you need. In addition, lost paperwork or online submissions due to the postal system, reporting systems, and payroll departments are another reason to keep copies of your paperwork. On all jobs, keep a copy of the sign-off sheet that has the store employee's signature, the confirmation number given when reporting completion via phone or web, timesheets, invoices and pay stubs when received. By keeping copies of the above information, you can prove the work you completed and keep your pay coming in. You can staple all these together in a file folder for each company you work for. Also, keep contact info and whatever else you decide is worth keeping.

Sometimes it is a good idea to keep pertinent instructions for the projects too. If you do service for a particular client on an ongoing basis, then you have previous notes and instruction on what you have already done. You may find it helpful to refresh your memory about a project before going back into a store.

If working as an independent contractor, then keep the paperwork and your e-mails that show how much pay is to be received for each project. This helps cut down on the company forgetting that they promised you a certain amount as payment.

But you are still required to file a Schedule C for your total IC income from all companies that you worked for even if you make less than $600 and don't receive the 1099. In fact, you are to file a Schedule C no matter how little your yearly total IC income is.

If you have unreimbursed expenses, then keep receipts or proof for these too so you can deduct them on your Schedule C at tax time. Many expenses such as postage, office supplies, fax fees, mileage, long-distance calls, and more are deductible when working as an independent contractor.

Collecting and keeping your records organized throughout the year will make tax time much easier. Business forms for mileage, invoice, and assignment log are available in the Appendix 3: Business Forms in the back pages folder. These helpful forms will keep you organized and give you a better idea of how your business is shaping up.

Five simple steps to maintaining organization of your records

Step number 1: Toss what you can.

Nearly all your financial papers can be divided into three categories:

1. Records that you need to keep only for the calendar year or less.
2. Papers that you need to save for seven years (the typical window during which your tax return may be audited).
3. Papers that you should hang onto indefinitely.

Don't keep sales receipts for minor purchases after you've satisfactorily used the item a few times or the warranty has expired.

Shortly after the end of the calendar year, you will probably be able to throw out a slew of additional paper including your paycheck stubs, monthly credit card, and mortgage statements, utility bills (if they are not needed for business deductions).

Step number 2: Hang on to what you must.

You will, however, need to hold on to those final credit card statements along with your W-2s and 1099s for at least three years and preferably, for seven.

For insurances purposes, you'll also want to keep receipts for major purchases and receipts that show how much you've paid for home improvements indefinitely, both to satisfy potential buyers and to reduce possible capital-gains taxes when you sell your home.

Step number 3: Give your papers a home.

Use a drawer, cabinet, or closet where you can store bills and current records, situated near a table on which you can write checks. As for supplies, you'll find that folders or manila envelopes will come in handy for filing the papers, as will a file cabinet or cardboard box to hold the records.

Step number 4: Be systematic.

Have a plan for processing all paper. Pick a spot in your information area where you'll put the bills—say a manila envelope, a drawer, or a plastic in-box—and toss in each envelope as it arrives in the mail. Then when you sit down to write those checks each month, you'll have all the paperwork you need in one spot.

Step number 5: Tackle the backlog.

Once you have a system in place, start by sorting through a small stack at a time. You can allot half an hour a day to sift through old papers, perhaps while watching the news or listening to music.

You'll be amazed at the difference a little organization makes!

APPENDIX 1

Interior Photographs

Illustrations included in this publication. These photos were made by the author.

1. Bar Code on Packaging
2. Four Components of UPC number
3. Table Showing Category Each UPC System Number Represents
4. Shelf Label
5. Examples of a Shelf Label and Product Packaging UPC
6. The Stock Number (Ordering or Store Item Number)
7. Date Printed on Label
8. Labels may show how product is ordered.
9. Handheld Scanner (Telxon, 960 unit, LRT, RMU)
10. Greeting Card Fixture
11. Base of a Shelving Unit
12. Pegboard
13. Gridwall
14. Slatwall
15. Uniweb
16. Upright Bars are on Back Wall of Shelving Unit
17. Shelves
18. Channel Moldings
19. Fencing
20. Riser
21. Cheater Shelf
22. Peg Hooks
23. Plastic Overlay for Peg Hooks
24. Snap Railing
25. J-Hook
26. Sidekick (Powerwing)

27. Clip Strip
28. Shelf Strips (Channel Strips)
29. Shelf Talker Bean Flip, Shelf Tag
30. Header Cards
31. Endcap
32. Dump Table (Dump Bin)
33. Countertop Display (Checkout Display)
34. Rolling Rack
35. Cross Merchandising
36. Acrylic Trays
37. 4-Way
38. Floor Display
39. Island Display
40. Spinner Rack

APPENDIX 2

Resources

A.I.M. Field Services, Apopka, FL, 800-881-5305, 407-886-5365, Web site: *www.patsaim.com*.

Acosta Sales and Marketing Co., Jacksonville, FL, 888-281-9800, Web site: *www.acosta.com*.

Action Merchandising, LLC, Frisco, TX, 800-673-6985, Web site: *www. actionmerchandising.com*.

ActionLink, Akron, OH, 888-737-8757, Web site: *www.actionlink.com*, Formerly Service Plus.

Advanced Retail Merchandising, Inc., Lakeland, FL, 800-229-1ARM, Web site: *www.arm-retail.com*.

Advantage Sales & Marketing, Irvine, CA, 949-797-2900, Web site: *www. asmnet.com*.

Aisle One Merchandising, Brea, CA, 714-986-1515, Web site: *www.aisleone. com*.

Alliance Marketing Group, LLC, Cordova, TN, 866-221-1797, Web site: *www.amgatretail.com*.

American Merchandising Specialists, Inc., Brentwood, CA, 925-516-3220, Web site: *www.merchandisers.net*.

Apollo Retail Specialists, Apollo Beach, FL, Web site: *www.apolloretail.com*.

Associated Merchandising Services, Plano, TX, 972-618-0938, Web site: *www.associatedmerchandisingservices.com.*

At Your Service Marketing, Chico, TX, 940-644-2893, 800-410-5396, Web site: *http://www.aysm.com/,*

ATA Retail Services, Inc., Hayward, CA, 800-287-1604, Web site: *www.ataretail.com.*

Atlantic Coast Merchandising LLC, Burgaw, NC, 910-300-9231, Web site: *www.acmerchandising.net.*

Baker & Taylor, Charlotte, NC, 949-472-6700, Web site: *www.btol.com.*

bds mktg, Irvine, CA, 630-235-5811, Web site: *www.bdsmktg.com.*

Berends Trading Company, Fort Wayne, IN, 260-485-2010, Web site: *www.berends-usa.com.*

Berglund & Associates, Minneapolis, MN, 952-746-4500, Web site: *www.BerglundandAssociates.com.*

Best Service Merchandising, Inc., New Berlin, WI, 262-349-9400.

Browns Merchandising & Demos, Arlington, 901-373-3066, Web site: *www.brownsretailservices.com.*

Campaigners, Inc., El Segundo, CA, 310-643-7500, 888-524-9192, Web site: *www.campaigners.com.*

Channel Partners, Irvine, CA, 949-472-6711, Web site: *www.channelpartners.com.*

ChannelForce, Gladstone, OR, 503-657-1600, Web site: *www.channelforce.com.*

Chuck Latham Associates, Inc., Parker, CO, 800-249-3768, Web site: *www.clareps.com.*

JUDITH ADKINS-SPEARS

Convergence Marketing, Hanover, MD, 443-688-5100, Web site: *www. convergencemktg.com.*

Courtland Associates, Inc., Farmington, MI, 800-847-2877, Web site: *www. courtlandmi.com.*

CPM-US LLC, Dallas, TX, 800-648-0722 X2702, Web site: *www. us.cpm-int.com.* (acquired National In-Store (NIS) in 2009).

Crane Sales Co., Tampa, FL, 813-806-9604.

Creative Agency Services Team, Inc., Sarasota, FL, 877-550-2278, Web site: *www.castretail.com.*

CROSSMARK Australia Pty Limited, Artarmon, NSW, 61 2 9439 1233.

CROSSMARK Canada, Mississauga, ON, 905-507-6222.

CROSSMARK Sales and Marketing, Inc., Plano, TX,888-366-3275, Web site: *www.crossmark.com.*

CSN Retail Services, Roseville, MN, 612-616-4013.

Dan Davis Enterprise Inc., Hesperia, CA, 760-241-2122.

DAVACO, Inc., Dallas, TX, 877-732-8226, Web site: *www.davacoinc. com.*

DisplayMax, Inc., Howell, MI,810-494-0400, Web site: *www. displaymaxmerchandising.com.*

Distribution Services Inc. (DSI), West Palm Beach, FL, 800-253-2955, Web site: *www.DistributionServices.com.*

Done Right Merchandising, Mooresville, NC, 704-662-7183, Web site: *www.donerightmerchandising.com.*

DP Merchandising Services, LLC, Sioux Falls, SD, 605-201-9234.

Driveline Retail Merchandising, Inc., Taylorville, IL, 763-553-3800, Web site: *www.drivelineretail.com.*

Driveline Retail Services LLC, Mooresville, NC, 800-892-9691, Web site: *www.drivelineinstore.com.*

DVDXPRESS, Avon, OH, 310-691-6048.

Eastern Retail Services, Hanover, VA, 804-730-1869, Web site: *www.easternretailservices.com.*

Ex-Sell Sales & Merchandising, Oakville, ON, 416-418-8602, Web site: *www.ex-sell.com.*

FHI Retail, Fuquay-Varina, NC, 800-849-3132, Web site: *www.freighthandlers.com.*

Finta LLC, Munroe Falls, OH, 330-721-6737, Web site: *www.fintaonline.com.*

First Choice Sales and Marketing Group, Memphis, TN, 901-360-8967, Web site: *www.firstchoicesale.com.*

Footprint Retail Services, Lisle, IL, 800-747-2257, Web site: *www.fprs.com.*

Franklin Resource Group, Inc., Boulder, CO, 303-282-3945, Web site: *www.FranklinResource.com.*

FSA Merchandising Inc., Delafield, WI, 262-646-7034, Web site: *www.fsaautomotive.co.uk.*

Garden Merchandising Inc., Perkasie, PA, 215-257-9001, Web site: *www.gardenmerchandising.net.*

Gardenvision, Goulds, FL, 305-247-3248.

Global Distribution Services, Irvine, CA, 949-855-8822.

Greet America, Inc., Lancaster, TX, 800-366-9822, Web site: *www. greetamerica.com.*

Griffin Sales & Service, L.L.C., Stockbridge, GA, 770-507-9573, Web site: *www.gssmerch.net.*

HDA Merchandising, St. Louis, MO, 800-367-0921, Web site: *www. hdamerchandising.com.*

Hispanic Indoor Media, Inc., Coarsegold, CA, 559-246-4895, Web site: *www.hispanicindoor.com.*

Horta Merchandising, Inc., London, ON, 866-560-5072.

In-Store Marketing, Inc., Charlotte, NC, 877-288-7886, Web site: *www. in-storemktg.com.*

In-Store Opportunities, Middletown, CT, 800-733-2999, Web site: *www. superfridge.com.*

InstalledByDeluxe.com, Norwalk, OH, 800-678-2757, Web site: *www. InstalledByDeluxe.com.*

Island In-Store Services, Inc., San Juan, PR, 787-273-1871.

J.R. Demos and Merchandising, Cincinnati, OH, 513-242-6700, Web site: *www.jrdemos.com.*

JO'H Eagle, Billerica, MA, 978-663-9000, Web site: *www.johare.com.*

Karpata Instore Service, Grand Rapids, MI, 616-791-0701, Web site: *www. meijerservice.com.* (dedicated solely to Meijer, Inc.)

Lawrence Merchandising Services, Plymouth, MN, 763-383-5701, Web site: *www.lmsvc.com.*

Levy Merchandising Services, Oak Brook, IL, 800-947-1967, Web site: *www.levyservices.com.*

M3 Merchandising, Wilmington, MA, 978-296-2632.

MAP (Multi-Merchandising Action Professionals), New Oxford, PA, 717-624-4405, Web site: *www.mapmerchandising.com.*

MarketSource, Inc., Alpharetta, GA, 877-494-4270 or 800-675-6685, Web site: *www.marketsource.net.*

Matrix Merchandising, Goulds, FL, 866-267-1794.

MCA-Merchandising Consultants Associates, Woodbridge, ON, 905-850-5544, Web site: *www.mca.ca.*

MCG—Market Connect Group, Bloomfield, NJ,973-337-4015, Web site: *www.mcgconnect.com.*

Merchandise & Audit Services, Inc., Rio Piedras, PR, 787-622-0870.

Merchandise Management Company, Brookfield, WI, 800-916-7076, Web site: *www.merchmanco.com.* (Services vendors for Kohl's Department stores, exclusively)

Merchandisers Unlimited, Inc., Jacksonville, FL, 800-848-9323, Web site: *www.merchunlimited.com.*

Merchandising Solutions Group, Inc., Hays, NC, 336-696-4209, Web site: *www.merchandisingsol.com.*

Mercury Retail Services, San Antonio, TX, 210-662-3329, Web site: *www. mercretail.com.*

Mosaic, Irving, TX,877-870-4800, Web site: *www.mosaic.com.*

Mosaic Sales Solutions—Canada, Mississauga, ON, 905-238-8422, Web site: *www.mosaic.com.*

MTI (Merchandising Technologies, Inc.), Hillsboro, OR, 503-648-6500, Web site: *www.mti-interactive.com.*

mVentix, Inc., Santa Clarita, CA,888-455-2341, Web site: *www.mventix. com.*

National Merchandising, Fayetteville, GA, 770-715-1153, Web site: *www. natlmerchandising.com.*

National Product Services, Inc., Irving, TX, 972-373-9484, Web site: *www. npsinet.com.*

News America Marketing, Wilton, CT,651-437-5112, Web site: *www. newsamerica.com.*

North America Merchandising Services, Canada, ULC, Calgary, AB, 403-313-9106, Web site: *www.namsicanada.com.*

Orion Sales Group, Toronto, ON, 416-521-9922, Web site: *www.orionsg. com.*

Pankow Associates—Mid-Atlantic Region, Skokie, IL, 847-679-7010.

Pat Henry Perceptions, Inc., Independence, OH, 800-229-5260 x212, Web site: *www.thepathenrygroup.com.*

Plant Partners, Huntersville, NC, 888-628-3958, Web site: *www. plant-partners.com.*

Platinum Service-Detail for Retail, LLC, Allendale, MI, 866-943-3824, Web site: *www.detailforretail.com or www.platinumservicellc.com.*

Precision Store Works, Epsom, NH, 603-736-9191.

Premier Workforce, Cornelius, NC, 704-897-8944, Web site: *www. premierworkforce.com.*

Premium Retail Services, Inc., Chesterfield, MO, 800-800-7318, Web site: *www.premiumretail.com.*

Prism Japan, Chiba-shi, Chiba, 81-43-350-4170.

Prism Retail Services a Division of Footprint Retail Services, Itasca, IL, 800-808-1992, Web site: *www.prismretailservices.com.*

Pro's Choice Beauty Care, Inc., Bellport, NY, 800-676-5554.

Professional Remerchandising Organization, Mooresville, NC, 877-583-3448.

Promotion Network, Inc., Palos Heights, IL, 708-361-8747.

ProVantage Corporate Solutions, Raleigh, NC, 919-600-6160, Web site: *www.provantage-corp.com.*

Quality First Merchandisers, Inc., Murrieta, CA, 951-894-1740.

Quest Service Group, LLC, Garden City, NY, 516-594-4400, Web site: *www.Questservicegroup.com.*

Quick Turn Merchandising, Fort Worth, TX, 866-339-2249, Web site: *www.qturns.com.*

ReAct Merchandising, Kansas City, MO, 913-568-4801, Web site: *www.reactmerchandising.com.*

Reliable Recruiters, LLC, Minneapolis, MN, 800-728-8141, Web site: *www.reliablerecruiters.com.*

Resource Plus, Inc., Jacksonville, FL, 888-678-8966, Web site: *www.resourcep.com.*

Retail Assistance Corporation, Scottsdale, AZ, 888-472-6033, Web site: *www.retailassistance.com.*

Retail Detail Merchandising, Inc., Altamonte Springs, FL, 407-774-6664, Web site: *www.rdmerchandising.com.*

Retail Integrity Merchandising Solutions Inc., Rogers, AR, 479-986-0736, Web site: *www.retailintegrity.com.*

Retail Marketing Professionals, Inc., Duluth, GA, 800-272-5534, Web site: *www.rmp-merchandising.com.*

Retail Merchandising Services Inc., Plymouth, MN, 800-777-3767, Web site: *www.rmservicing.com.*

Retail Merchandising Solutions Inc., Livermore, CA, 503-678-3349, Web site: *www.rmsicorp.com.*

Retail Service Partners, Shillington, PA, 717-479-0205, Web site: *www.retailservicepartners.com.*

Retail Services Inc., Overland Park, KS, 913-383-0411, Web site: *www.4rsi.com.*

Retail Services, LLC, 616-957-4424, Web site: *www.retailsvcs.com.*

Revenue Creations, Suffern, NY, 845-357-3343.

Rhodes Retail Services, Inc., Elk Grove, CA, 866-714-9233, Web site: *www.rhodesretail.com.*

RitterAssociates, Inc., Toledo, OH, 419-535-5757, Web site: *www.ritterassociates.com.*

Riverhook Retail Group, Kansas City, MO, 816-531-2766.

RNFB, Inc., Joplin, MO, 866-566-6590, Web site: *www.qualityroadshows.com.*

Rocky Mountain Merchandising & Services, Salt Lake City, UT, 801-274-0220, Web site: *www.rockymm.com.*

Sales Edge, Wytheville, VA, 888-566-7253, Web site: *www.salesedgeservice.com.*

SAS ROI Retail Merchandising, Orange, CA, 800-649-1075, Web site: *www.sasmerchandising.com.*

Select Media Services, Duluth, GA, 888-236-9457, Web site: *www. selectmediaservices.com.*

Sell-Thru Services, Inc., Austin, TX, 800-234-7874, Web site: *www.sell-thru. com.*

Set and Service Resources, LLC, Raleigh, NC, 919-787-5571, Web site: *www.sasrlink.com.*

Shelf Tech, Little Falls, NJ, 973-237-9595, Web site: *www.shelftech.com.*

Signature Retail Services, Lombard, IL, 630-678-1212, Web site: *www. signatureretailservices.com.*

SMMC, Lawrenceville, GA, 800-932-4276.

Source Interlink Companies, Bonita Springs, FL, 239-949-4450, Web site: *www.sourceinterlink.com.*

SPAR Canada & SPAR Wings & Ink, Vaughan, ON, 888-535-5710, Web site: *www.sparinc.com.*

SPAR Group, Inc., Tarrytown, NY, 914-332-4100, Web site: *www.sparinc. com.*

SPARFACTS Australia P/L, Melbourne State, VIC, 61 3 9376 2255.

Specialized Merchandising Services, Williamsville, NY, 716-884-6901 x122.

Specialty Store Services, Thornton, CO, 303-587-7706 x237.

Stan Tashman & Associates, Culver City, CA, 800-767-4071.

Store Opening Solutions Retail Services, LLC, Murfreesboro, TN, 615-867-0858.

Strategic Retail Solutions, Rocky River, OH, 440-356-4660.

StratMar Retail Services, Port Chester, NY, 914-937-7171 x 405, Web site: *www.stratmar.com.*

Summit Services Unlimited, Inc., Williamsville, NY, 800-261-7080, Web site: *www.ssuretail.com.*

Surge Merchandising Inc., Greenville, SC, 864-232-7362.

SymphonyIRI Group, Inc., Chicago, IL, Web site: *www.infores.com.*

The Eleven Agency, Irvine, CA, 949-679-1182, Web site: *www.theelevenagency.com.*

The Merchandising Team, Bloomington, MN, 888-777-4747, Web site: *www.themerchandisingteam.com.*

The North 51st Group Inc., Mississauga, ON, 905-629-2224, Web site: *www.north51.com.*

The Pet Firm, Phoenix, AZ, 602-648-2261, Web site: *www.thepetfirm.com.*

Time Is Money Merchandising Company, West Chester, PA, 610-715-1724.

Time Warner Retail Sales & Marketing, Parsippany, NJ, 973-939-7259, Web site: *www.Time.com.*

Total Merchandising Services, Newaygo, MI, 231-652-1776.

Total Service Company, Brentwood, TN, 615-377-2377.

TouchPoint 360, LLC, Mount Prospect, IL, 800-460-8177, Web site: *www.touchpoint360.com.*

TrendSource, Inc., San Diego, CA, 619-718-7467, Web site: *www.trendsource.com.*

Turns Service and Assembly Inc., Atlanta, GA, 678-249-7450, Web site: *www.turnsinc.com.*

Universal Sales, Kalamazoo, MI, 269-381-9734.

Williams Creative Group, Inc., Brentwood, TN, 888-346-6011, Web site: *www.williamscreativegroup.net.*

WIS Merchandising and Retail Services, Lutz, FL,813-864-2889, Web site: *www.wisintl.com.*

Wolfe Retail Services, Inc., Brookfield, WI, 800-345-9227, Web site: *www.wolferetail.com.*

WorkSmart Merchandising, Greenville, SC, 888-246-2988, Web site: *www.wsmerchandising.com.*

Zoom Eyeworks Inc., Berkeley, CA, 800-393-9273, Web site: *www.zoomeyeworks.com.*

APPENDIX 3

Business Forms

1. List of Companies to Which You Applied

COMPANIES TO WHICH YOU APPLY

Date: .... Company Name: ....
Mailing Address: ....
Contact Phone: .... Fax Number: ....
Website Address: ....
Email Address: ....
Scheduler/ Notes: ....
....
....

Date: .... Company Name: ....
Mailing Address: ....
Contact Phone: .... Fax Number: ....
Website Address: ....
Email Address: ....
Scheduler/ Notes: ....
....
....

Date: .... Company Name: ....
Mailing Address: ....
Contact Phone: .... Fax Number: ....
Website Address: ....
Email Address: ....
Scheduler/ Notes: ....
....
....

Date: .... Company Name: ....
Mailing Address: ....
Contact Phone: .... Fax Number: ....
Website Address: ....
Email Address: ....
Scheduler/ Notes: ....
....
....

Date: .... Company Name: ....
Mailing Address: ....
Contact Phone: .... Fax Number: ....
Website Address: ....
Email Address: ....
Scheduler/ Notes: ....
....
....

Date: .... Company Name: ....
Mailing Address: ....
Contact Phone: .... Fax Number: ....
Website Address: ....
Email Address: ....
Scheduler/ Notes: ....
....
....

2. Information on Each Company

COMPANY COVER SHEET

Company Name: ....

Mailing Address: ....

....

....

Contact Phone: .... Contact Person: ....

Fax Number: .... Hours of Operation: ....

Website Address: ....

Opportunities
Webpage: ....

App. Accepted
& Approved: ....

Personal ID #: ....

Specialty: ....

Notes: ....

....

....

....

....

....

....

....

3. Shop Assignment Log

ASSIGNMENT LOG

Use this log to keep track of your assignments and paychecks.

COMPANY	ASSIGN DATE	LOCATION	CONTRACT $	DATE PAID

4. Mileage Log

MILEAGE LOG

Use this log to keep track of your mileage.

DATE	COMPANY	STARTING ODOMETER READING	ENDING ODOMETER READING	TOTAL MILES DRIVEN	LESS VARIANCE	MINUS PERSONAL MILES	PAYABLE MILES	COMMENTS

JUDITH ADKINS-SPEARS

5. Invoice Log

INVOICE

DATE	CLIENT	COMPANY	JOB #	LABOR	EXPENSES	TOTAL DUE	COMMENTS

6. Password List

MERCHANDISING LOG-IN INFO SHEET							
COMPANY NAME	URL ADDRESS	SIGN-UP DATES				USER NAME	PASSWORD

APPENDIX 4

Application Examples

Chronological Resume

YOUR NAME
Your Address
Your City, State Zip Code
Your Phone Number
Your Email Address

Objectives   One sentence statement that provides your "objective" for applying for the job.

Work History

07/25/98 -Present   *Human Resources Assistant Manager*, ABC Retail, Tuscan, Arizona
- Assists Human Resources Manager in monitoring job openings, screening applicants, interviewing applicants, closing and status of job openings including background checks and exit interviews.
- Conduct Orientation and schedule Register Training classes for all New Hires.
- Compensations and Benefits

01/92-Present   *Merchandiser*, MarketingUSA, Bigtown, TX
- Gas Stations, Grocery, and Retail stores.

06//98-12/98   *Merchandiser*, Merchandising USA, Littletown, Utah
- Retail, Home Improvement, and Gas Stations.

06/98-07/98   *Sales Executive,* Freightway USA, Honolulu, Hawaii
- Assigned local territories, look for and gain new accounts, develop and maintain existing accounts consistent with company policy and objectives.
- Maintained current and accurate weekly and monthly sales reports and answer all sales leads and other correspondence promptly.

Education

California State University of Hayward, Hayward California
Bachelor of Science in Business Administration with a Major in Marketing Management
And a minor in Communication Skills

Personal Accomplishments/Affiliations

- Associated Vice President for Fund Raising, Advertising, and Public Relations, PI SIGMA EPSILON, Professional Marketing Fraternity
- California Real Estate License
- Active Member of the National Center for Professional Mystery Shoppers, Inc.
- General Excise License
- Windows 98 and ME

Functional Format Resume

YOUR NAME
Your Address
Your City, State Zip Code
Your Phone Number
Your Email Address

Objectives   One sentence statement that provides your "objective" for applying for the job.

Work History
Human Resources Assistant Manager, ABC Retail, Tuscan, Arizona
- Assists Human Resources Manager in monitoring job openings, screening applicants, interviewing applicants, closing, and status of job openings including background checks and exit interviews.
- Conduct Orientation and schedule Register Training classes for all New Hires.
- Compensations and Benefits

Merchandiser, MarketingUSA, Bigtown, TX
- Gas Stations, Grocery, and Retail stores.

Merchandiser, Merchandising USA, Littletown, Utah
- Retail, Home Improvement, and Gas Stations.

Sales Executive, Freightway USA, Honolulu, Hawaii
- Assigned local territories, look for and gain new accounts, develop and maintain existing accounts consistent with company policy and objectives.
- Maintained current and accurate weekly and monthly sales reports and answer all sales leads and other correspondence promptly.

Flex-Schedule Teller, ABC Bank, San Jose, California
- Handled all basic financial transaction for customers; cash checks, deposits, withdrawals, account inquiries, merchant accounts, including credit card and loan payments and inquiries, using 10-key calculator and computer system.
- Balanced cash drawer and transactions; sort, file, and encode checks; money orders, travelers checks, and cashier's check.
- Customer Service, trained new employees, verified cash tills, and extensive cash handling.

Education
California State University of Hayward, Hayward California
> Bachelor of Science in Business Administration with a Major in Marketing Management
>> And a minor in Communication Skills

Personal Accomplishments/Affiliations
- Associated Vice President for Fund Raising, Advertising, and Public Relations, PI SIGMA EPSILON, Professional Marketing Fraternity
- California Real Estate License
- Active Member of the National Center for Professional Merchandisers, Inc.
- General Excise License

Jane E. Doe

Your Address
Your City, State Zip Code
Your Phone Number
Your Email Address

OBJECTIVE

To acquire a Merchandising position with a national firm.

AVAILABILITY

Currently available to cover the surrounding cities including Wallace, Lenten, Barry, Camp Paris, Bay Faults, and Rick, California.

ACHIEVEMENTS & QUALIFICATIONS

Nominated 2000 Merchandiser of the Year
Over 3 years experience as a Professional Merchandiser
Computer literate in popular software programs including Microsoft Office and Works.

AFFILIATIONS

National Center for Professional Merchandisers
American Business Women Association
National Association for Secretaries
Mission Volunteers Inc.

EDUCATION & CERTIFICATIONS

Win Academy, Mission, CA. (1999). Bachelors of Marketing
Mission College, Mission, CA. (1996). Studied Technical Writing
Shell Community College, Wallace, CA. (1993). AA Liberal Arts

MYSTERY SHOPPING EXPERIENCE

2000- Present	ABC Merchandisers	Retail and Gas Stations
1999- Present	XYZ Merchandisers	Retail and Grocery
1999- Present	SAVE Merchandisers	Retail and Clothing
1999- Present	TRY Merchandisers	Retail and Home Improvement
1997- Present	DERBY Marketing	Automotive and Electronic
1997- 2000	Keep Customers	Office Supplies and Electronic
1997- 1998	Cameo Marketing	Electronic and Retail
1996- 2000	Do It Marketing	Automotive and Electronic
1996- 1999	REAL Merchandisers	Retail and Clothing
1995- 1999	JR & Associates	Home Improvement
1995- 1998	Professional You	Retail and Gas Stations
1994- 1998	Cross Marketing	Retail and Grocery
1994- 1997	Progress Marketing	Retail and Clothing

OTHER EXPERIENCE

Peterson Distribution, Mission, CA (1997- Present) **Front Desk Manager**
Process technical reports and claims. Type and file all documents for staff of 15 licensed professionals. Coordinate all staff meetings, answer all incoming calls, and arrange courier deliveries.

Carlton Bank, Mission, CA (1993- 1997)   **Loan Secretary**
Prepared all loan documents for review. Managed training of new secretaries. Acted as a liaison between customers and loan officers. Monitored banking supplies, office equipment, and repair request.

YOUR NAME
Your Address
Your City, State Zip Code
Your Phone Number
Your Email Address

Date

Name
Title
Organization
Address
City, State Zip Code

Dear Mr./Mrs. Last Name:

First Paragraph: Why You Are Writing. Remember to include the name of a mutual contact, if you have one. Be clean and concise regarding your request.

Middle Paragraphs: What You Have to Offer. Convince the readers that they should grant the interview or appointment you requested in the first paragraph. Make connections between your abilities and their needs or your need for information and their ability to provide it. Remember, you are interpreting your resume. Try to support each statement you make with a piece of evidence. Use several shorter paragraphs rather than one large block of text.

Final Paragraph: How You Will Follow Up. Remember, it is your responsibility to follow-up; this relates to your job search. State that you will do so and provide the professional courtesy of indicating when (one week's time is typical). You may want to reduce the time between sending out your resume and follow up if you fax or e-mail it.

Sincerely,

Your Signature

Your Typed Name

GLOSSARY

Accessories: Items that coordinate with a basic article of clothing to make it more appealing; it includes items such as gloves, stockings, scarves.

Account: A group of stores that are customers of the same company

Account Number: A six-, eight-, or ten-digit number that identifies the account

Acknowledgment: An acknowledgment from a store associate is a type of recognition that you have entered the establishment. This can be verbal or nonverbal (i.e., a nod of the head).

Acrylic Trays: Made of hard clear plastic and are typically used to build cosmetic sets.

Action Alley (A/A): The main aisleway that runs around the store. Referred to by location, such as back-action alley, front-action alley, etc. (Wal-Mart—Action Alley; Kmart—Midway; Target—Racetrack).

Addition/Deletion: Items that will be added to or deleted from a planogram during a reset

Add-on: Additional merchandise that could be added to a sale and purchased by the customer

Adjacent: Merchandise of departments that are next to or nearby each other, such as Hair Shampoos are adjacent to Hair Conditioners.

Adjacent Stockroom: See *stockroom*

Adjacency: The layout of the store that shows how each planogram or rack is set next to each other.

Aging: The length of time that goods have been left in stock

AIM: Automatic Inventory Management

Air Space: Too much space between products, rows, shelves, etc.

Aisle: Sections of shelving units placed together to display product that the store normally carries

Aisle Advertising: A store item display used to attract attention and make the item accessible to purchasers; it usually has the same copy and graphics used in other promotional efforts produced by the sponsoring product. See *POP advertising*.

Allocate: To assign space on the shelf for products; it is based on product movement and other measures.

Allocation: A limited quantity of merchandise that is ordered and sent to the stores, usually less than a full order.

Alpha Box: A clear-locking security box used on SKUs over $50 to prevent theft, or in high theft stores, on any SKU the MOD feels is needed. It can be pegged or sat on a shelf.

Answer/Response: The basic answers to questions on the questionnaire—usually in the form of Yes/No/Not Applicable, numeric, or from options, e.g., A, B, C, etc., where each letter represents a specific type of occurrence.

Apron: An open area within the store where displays are set on freestanding units or built entirely of items from the floor up

Assembly: Program by which certain items in the store are ordered. An assembly item comes directly from the vendor to the warehouse and then to the store.

Assortment: Various forms of the same general type of item, such as the depth and width of the merchandise offering. *Depth* is about variety, an array of styles, colors, and prices; *width* is about different product categories such as towels, hats, lotions to accompany the sale of bathing suits.

Attend and Assist: To attend a remodel or new store set up and (A/A) assist as instructed

Attribute: A desired quality considered as belonging to a person or thing. A characteristic.

Audit: (1) An examination and verification of anything from quantity, availability, or pricing; (2) overt or covert visits by representatives who are asked to check merchandising and point-of-purchase issues, including, but not limited to, the stocking, placement, and pricing of specific merchandise and POP materials. Usually requested to ensure policy compliance by either a retail store or the manufacturer of the product.

Authorized Stock Item (a.k.a. Traited item or In-Distribution Product): An item stocked by a chain or affiliated retailer, which has been approved for space on the shelf by the chain or wholesale-buying headquarters. See *Traited*.

Automatic Distribution: A method employed by chain headquarters and wholesale grocers to cover key stores promptly by allotting and delivering new items, current deals and special promotion stock to retail stores without specific order from the store manager.

Automatic Replenishment: The ordering of product as it sells. See *replenishment, POS, or AIM*.

Back Card: A printed large card designed to fit on the back of a display bin or a pole describing the special offer being displayed.

Back Order: An item or order that is presently not in stock but is being reordered and will be available at another time. Product that was ordered and not included with shipment. Will be shipped when available.

Back Room: Stockroom or receiving area where reserve product is stored

Backstock: Additional merchandise available in the stockroom or warehouse

Back Tag: A printed card that hangs from the back of a peg hook. This helps identify what goes on a particular peg if there is an out-of-stock situation. This could also be in the form of a sticker on the peg.

Back-up Card: A card placed on a pegboard hook or on pegboard indicating size, number, selling price, and other information concerning the item that will be displayed at that spot.

Back Wall: The farthest backboard of a wall or gondola section. It can be pegboard, gridwall, or slatwall.

Bagel: Round plastic markers fitting on hanger rods. They identify clothing by size.

Baler: A large cardboard compactor found in the backroom

Banana Box: A box that is used to ship bananas. These boxes are used to pack or repack discontinued and/or not in set items.

Banded Pack: Items offered at retail that are secured by a tape, string, or plastic filmstrip and, therefore, sold as one unit.

Banner: Usually a plastic or cloth rectangle with grommets in the corners, designed to be suspended from the ceiling or between posts.

Bar Code: A group of lines printed on a piece of merchandise or on a label attached to the merchandise, also known as a UPC Code.

Bar Code Scanners: Reads bar codes. Bar code scanners are generally classified as wands, handhelds, etc.

Base: The bottom flat shelf of each shelving unit that never changes position, the next shelf up is referred to as Shelf 1.

Base Wrap: A continuous roll of paper, normally with product illustrations, used to conceal the bottom cases of a mass display.

Bay: Large open areas that sometimes run the length of an aisle where oversize product is located for sale with each product having its own "bay." The area of placement is according to a POG.

Bayonet/Backer Card: A plastic card that is placed behind the product that shows the Title/UPC, and in most cases, price (is not necessary per a POG can be used as a sales tag holder also).

Beam Flip: The plastic piece that holds up the rollback sign at Wal-Mart

Blister Pack: A package in which an item(s) of merchandise is covered with a transparent plastic casing and attached to a piece of cardboard.

Blitz: A type of merchandising that denotes a rapid rollout of a product or planogram within a geographic area. A blitz is usually coordinated in a compressed time frame on a given initiative, project, or circumstance. The time frame is less than a normal cycle, usually one or two weeks, in which service must be completed.

Blocking:

1. Product is evenly merchandised on the shelf.
2. Pulling product forward on the shelf.

BOGO: Buy One, Get One

BOGOF: Buy One, Get One Free

Bonus Pack: Special packaging that provides consumers with extra quantity of merchandise at no extra cost over a regular pack

Bottleneck: Displays placed at the end of shopping aisles allowing only one cart to pass at a time

Branch: The specific site that is visited or called—i.e., retail establishment, bank.

Branch Code: A number assigned to a particular branch that remains the same whenever that branch is visited

Brand: A name, mark, or symbol (or combination of these) that identifies the product or service offered by sellers.

Brand Partners: In Kmart, Vendors are referred to as Brand Partners.

Briefing Notes: Also called guidelines explains how to carry out any given shop.

Building a Display: Arranging and putting together merchandise or sample products, usually from scratch.

Bundle Packs: Several different products or units packaged together and sold as a single unit

Call: A visit to a store/client to complete work in that store

Call-Ins: Items the buyer has determined should be returned to a designated location

Call Report: A report filled out during a store visit to provide data to the client

Capacity: The number of items that can be stocked on the shelf or display when fully stocked (regardless of how many are actually present on the shelf). This is different than that of an inventory count.

Carded Product: Items packaged with a backing and clear front to allow customers to see the product. Products are usually merchandised on pegs. The "card" is a cardboard backer.

Case Out: When product is kept in its case (with one side of the case cut to reveal the product) when put on the shelf for sale

Case Pack: Each individual case of a certain product

Case Pack Out: Shelving term that describes when a full case of a product fits in the amount of shelf space allotted for that product.

Category:

1. A grouping of products that have a common consumer end use, e.g., pet foods.
2. Refers to the section (set) in the store, e.g., software, printers.

Cents-Off Coupon: A coupon that entitles the holder to a discount on merchandise at the time of purchase.

Chain: Organization with two or more centrally owned stores handling similar merchandise

Chain Drug Store: A pharmacy-driven outlet with a large general merchandise and HBA business, e.g., Walgreen's, Eckerds, CVS.

Channel Strips: An advertising message for shelf stock, affixed in the channel molding. See *Shelf Strips*.

Charge Back: When the store returns product to the warehouse, the store "charges" or requests reimbursement from the warehouse for the product they are returning. If the warehouse decides to deny the charge, for whatever reason, it is called a Charge Back.

Cheater Shelf: Flex space below the riser

Check Digit: The last digit of the UPC code is called a check digit and is the far right number on a product package

Check Lane Fixture: Fixtures at cash register inline or endcaps at the store

Checkout Counter: The location where items bought are checked and paid for; it is frequently used for point-of-sale displays.

Chinese Walls: (Slang) Imaginary barriers or false walls between a store's departments

Circular: A method of advertising. This is sometimes called Roto or Flyer.

Clamshell: The hard plastic casing/cover for videos used to prevent theft

Clearance Merchandise: Merchandise that the retailer has discontinued and cannot charge back to the manufacturer, usually seasonal and priced to sell quickly.

Client: The client is the manufacturer/distributor that contracts with the merchandising companies to employ merchandisers to represent/service their product at store level.

Clip Strip: A plastic strip used to hang merchandise in a secondary location, usually carded products. Clip strips are used to display high profit, impulse items that are displayed throughout the store. See *Product Clips.*

Close of Sale: A technique used by salespeople to complete a sale. Staff may be trained to finish a conversation in such a way as to try and encourage you to buy a particular product or service.

Closed Branch: If a branch was closed such that it could not be visited again during the wave, then it is designated a closed branch

Closed-Loop Layout: The placing of fixtures and aisles as incentives for the customer to move around the outer sections of the store. Synonymous with *racetrack layout.*

Closed Question: This is a question you might be asked by a member of the staff at a branch as part of a shop for which there is a finite and small number of possible responses. Opposite of Open Question.

Code Dating: Manufacturer's practice of marking a code on an item to determine the packer or to measure the salable life of an item

Coffin Case: A waist-high open-faced refrigerated or freezer case usually used for impulse or sale items

Collateral: Product signage added to enhance brand recognition. This can be located in the primary product display or in a secondary location.

Comment: Some responses ask for an additional explanation, e.g., if the response to "Were you greeted?" is yes, then you may be asked to state the exact greeting and who said it. Also some questions may be "comment only," i.e., if no response as outlined above is asked for, you just make a written comment.

Companion Goods: See *related merchandise*

Competition Markdown: A markdown taken on a particular product to meet a competitor's ad

Computerized Inventory System: A computer program that tracks inventory and sometimes creates automated replenishment orders

Corrugate: Cardboard display vehicle that is shipped with a new release or promotional item used to display the product. A corrugate can be a tray of a freestanding display

Counter: A table or top of a cabinet within the store that is used for the display and sale of items

Counter Card: A sign placed on a counter to advertise and promote an article for sale at that location. Counter cards may be with merchandise or to serve as a sales promotion/reminder.

Countertop Display: Prepackaged product (usually twelve to eighteen units) display designed to be placed on a counter with merchandising materials. Same as a *Counter Unit*.

Coupon: Sales promotion technique in which a consumer can redeem for a price reduction

Coverage: The extent to which a call/client is serviced. How long a merchandiser services a call in a store.

Cross-Aisle Merchandising: Displaying related merchandise on facing shelves

Cross Merchandising: A way of displaying and selling merchandising which does not traditionally sell together. A very effective way of increasing impulse purchases and displaying seasonal merchandise and new products, i.e., batteries on clip strips placed next to battery-operated toys.

Cut-Case Display: A product display created by trimming the corrugated outer casing to display the product contained within. Also called a *Punch Out*.

Cut-In: When a new product is introduced, the manufacturer usually likes to cut in the new product into the existing planogram via a revision; to place new items on an existing display, fixture, or shelf by removing old items or reducing the facings of existing items.

Cycle: A set time period during which a merchandising visit can be performed

Cycle Count: Inventories taken at store level to correct or update current on hand, usually using the store's Telzon Gun.

Damages:

1. Items available for sale in a damaged state, usually at a greatly reduced price.
2. Products that cannot be sold because it was damaged.

Dead Label: An EAS label in an inactive state where it will not alarm an EAS System

Dead Stock: Merchandise that cannot be sold.

Dedicated Service: Another word for exclusive service, loyal to one account/client.

Dedicated Space: Space in a store that has been purchased by a company to be used for displaying that company's product only

Deletes: Items that are no longer on the planogram/modular. See *discontinued or disco'd items*.

Demonstration: Showing how to complete a task. Sometimes called a demo, often used in conjunction with food sampling.

Department: The major subdivision within a store, either selling or nonselling, having a specialized function.

Department Manager (DM): The person in the department that is responsible for ordering, conducting markdowns, and overall management of the department.

Departmental Lead-In: Items with greatest impulse value are displayed on the edge of the shelf and near the main traffic aisle to draw customers into the aisle.

Departments: Specialized stores within a store such as Cosmetics, Grocery, Pet, Shoes, Apparel.

Depth: The number of distinct items within a product line

Descriptive Labeling:

1. Labeling that explains the important characteristics or benefits of a product.
2. The labeling of merchandise by characteristic but without considering grades or accepted standards.

Directs: Refers to

1. the area in receiving where merchandise that is shipped from the vendor is processed,
2. merchandise ordered by assembly or location,
3. purchase Order that is shipped directly from the vendor to the store.

Discontinued Items: Items that are no longer being merchandised in the category. See *Deletes*.

Disguised Retail Audit: An audit carried on without any awareness by the store's workers

Display:

1. Fixtures on which merchandise is placed in the stores. Displays differ based on their placement and type, e.g., window displays, floor displays, point-of-purchase advertising displays.
2. An entire gondola side, counter, category set complete with product and point-of-purchase materials.

Display Arrangement of Merchandise: Usually accompanied by printed signs. An entire gondola side, counter, category set complete with product and point-of-purchase materials.

Display Bin (Floor Stand): Folding cardboard display bin used for display of small items

Display Card: A tear-off card containing an advertisement that is affixed to a store display

Display Board: Board or panel displaying assembled merchandise. Shows customers how merchandise is used or how projects can be completed.

Display Material: Backboards, poles, posters, shelf cards, etc., made for product promotions.

Display Work: To build a special display yourself, or to check that it was built correctly and in the proper location by store personnel.

Disposable Label: An EAS label that is attached to or inserted inside of merchandise or packaging and is not intended to be removed at the point of purchase

Distressed Goods: Items that have been damaged or soiled

Distribute: To sell, promote, and ship merchandise.

Distribution: Seasonal merchandise sent automatically approximately each month

JUDITH ADKINS-SPEARS

Distribution Center: Where a store chain keeps product until an individual store places an order or the Perpetual Inventory System automatically replenishes

Distribution Void: Referred to as *void*. The item is authorized to be on the shelf, and is currently no shelf space, no shelf tag, and no product available for sale.

District Manager: Responsible for all activities in an assigned territory including hiring, training, and managing of Service Representatives.

Dividers: Placement of an item that is approximately three inches high. These are used along with fencing to separate small items on the shelves.

Do ITs: Plastic tabs that are used to repair damaged holes on hanging product packaging. See *Repair Tabs.*

Domestics: Yard goods from which sheets, linens, towels, and so on, are cut. Today, the term is more popularly identified with finished products.

Drop List: A list of deleted or discontinued items

Drop a Mod: In some stores, this is the phrase used to say the old planogram is being replaced by a new one.

Drop Shipment: Product sent to store using UPS or FedEx, instead of through the warehouse. Drop shipments are not always ordered by the stores. Some are "pushed" or forced through the manufacturer.

Direct-Store Delivery (DSD): Merchandise that is stocked by a store but is not ordered through the store. A vendor rep places the order, and the merchandise is then shipped direct from the manufacturer to the store, bypassing a wholesaler.

Direct-Store Door (DSD): These items are usually not inventoried by the store

Dummy Facings: When the actual product is not in stock, another product with the same dimensions is temporarily faced backward to ensure correct space is left on shelf.

Dump: Basket-type fixture used for displaying merchandising

Dump Bin / Speed Table: A store fixture or cardboard fixture that is table-like for displaying product

Dump Display: Goods that are casually tossed on a table or into a box, often to project a bargain image to customers

Dump Tables: Bulk display units in which fast-moving, impulse items can be "dumped" without stacking or placing on regular fixtures.

Duratrans: Product signage made of flexible plastic, which allows light to come through from behind the sign.

DV: Distribution Void. There is no product on the shelf and no tag either.

European Article Number (EAN): The European equivalent of the UPC. These thirteen-digit codes differ from their American counterpart by identifying country, manufacturer, item number, and check digit.

Electronic Article Surveillance (EAS) Label: A special tag attached and/or adhered to products, usually higher ticket items, which will set off an alarm when passed through EAS detection equipment.

Electronic Detection Device: An electronic tag that is affixed to an item which, if not properly removed at the point of sale, will trigger an alarm as the customer walks out of the store.

EDI: Acronym for Electronic Data Interchange ordering process

Electronic Tag Keys: A specially designed key that is used to move electronic tags during resets

Electronic Tags: A digital display unit attached through electrical connections to the price molding of the shelf, which displays the price of an item.

Elevation: The distance between one shelf and another, measured in two ways:

1. Top-to-Top: Elevations are measured from the top of the base to the top of the first shelf, top of the second shelf, etc.
2. Airspace: Elevations are measured from the top of the base to the bottom of the first shelf, top of the first shelf to the bottom of the second shelf, etc.

Empty Box Software: Empty software box in place of live product priced over $79.99

Endcap (E/C): High-traffic display area located at the end of an aisle that is designed to increase product movement. High margin items are placed on endcaps to generate impulse purchases.

End Display: A display with a considerable amount of goods set up at the end of a store aisle

End-Aisle Display: A point-of-purchase display of goods that is placed at the end of a row of shelving

Evaluate/Audit/Survey: To test an employee, product, or attribute

Exception: A situation or circumstance that does not conform to the standards relative to a store, section configuration, or other components.

Exclusive: Undivided loyalty to one client. Also known as dedicated service.

Expiration Date: A date printed or stamped on product when it is to be pulled from sales floor

Extender Shelf: A small shelf added to the molding. In the deli case, used for small promotional items.

Eye-Level Merchandising: Displaying the fastest selling and most profitable merchandise from waist to eye level—forty to sixty inches above the floor.

FIFO: "First In, First Out" means the rotation system in which the oldest stock is put on sale first.

Face Out:

1. A display fixture where goods, usually apparel, are hung so that they face out toward the customer.
2. Layout of the front row of all products as they will appear in the final set.

Facings:

1. The number of a product is merchandised on the shelf or peg hook. Some better-selling products have more than one facing.
2. Pulling product forward on the shelf.

False Face: Filling in empty hooks with like product to give the appearance of a full display until the next order arrives

Fast-Back: A metal two-prong hook used to hold pegs onto the pegboard. There are two types: 250 holds the standard pegs, and 212 holds the skinny pegs.

Fastag or Fact **Tag:** Chains' name for a plastic holder of product information and sometimes the reorder label that is affixed to the shelf in front of the product

Feature Ad: Primary sale ads that are regularly distributed by the chain

Fee: Payment due to a shopper for each shop completed

Fencing: A metal or acrylic rail secured to the front of the shelf to contain product on the shelf. Fencing is used almost always when slant shelves are being used.

Fill-Ins: Merchandise secured during a period of demand to replace those already sold to avoid lost sales of merchandise that is moving well

Fixture: A display furnishing to hold merchandise

JUDITH ADKINS-SPEARS

Fixture Accessory: Shelves, Peg Hooks, etc., that hold product.

Fixture Fill: Amount of product it takes to completely stock a shelf/fixture/display

Flex: A space that is not set to a schematic. This can be anything from an entire section to a row of pegs. This is where leftover promotions, clearance items, etc., can be placed. Oftentimes, new products are placed in flex areas until they can be cut into the actual modular.

Flip Flop: To exchange the placements of two pieces, or sections, of merchandise.

Floor Display: A freestanding self-contained merchandising display unit of product that sits on the sales floor. The merchandise may or may not be currently carried by the store on a routine basis.

Floor Stand: Large temporary display with a base that will stand on its own. Often, it is convertible to use as a power wing.

Floorset: Another name for a planogram

Fluff and Duff: An easy job consisting of cleaning and straightening and/or facing a product area

FOOS: Acronym for Fixed Out of Stock. The item was "out of stock" upon entry, and you were able to place product on the shelf for the consumer to purchase.

4-Way: A four-sided fixture used in Action alleys to feature merchandise; it can be pegged or shelved, modularized or flex.

Freestanding Store: A retail outlet that stands by itself and is not attached to a mall or shopping center

Frequency: Rate of occurrence of a merchandiser's visits

Front-End: The area where registers, service desk, and checkout tables are. Often refers to the wall of merchandise opposite of the registers.

Front-End Checkout: A store layout with check stands and registers at or near the store's entrance rather than throughout the store

Front of Store (FOS): The main aisle at the front of the store

Front Runner: Plastic strips attached to the pegs to hold the labels

Fronting: The daily merchandising action of pulling product to the front of the peg, shelf, hook, or display.

Freestanding Insert (FSI): Usually located in the Sunday paper, an ad usually containing a coupon

Garvey Gun: A handheld ticket gun used to price merchandise

General Merchandise (GM): The products that are sold in a mass merchandiser, supermarket, or drugstore, which are not grocery, meat, produce, or deli items. These GM products would include HBC, Hardware, software, etc. Also referred to as nonfoods or variety.

Gondola:

1. A type of freestanding shelving unit where products are merchandised, usually secured to the floor.
2. It is an island shelving unit open on all sides.
3. It is a secured upright fixture to which shelving is added.
4. These unit sections are placed side by side and are what form the aisles in the store.
5. High-profile gondolas are around seventy-two inches high and low-profile gondolas are forty-eight inches high.

Graphics: Signs to draw customer's attention to displays and identify product

Greeting: A greeting is a verbal acknowledgment that you have entered the branch location

Grid Layout: The placement of fixtures and aisles within the store; it is based on rectangles, squares, and other right-angle patterns.

Gross Floor Space: The total store area, including selling and nonselling departments.

Grouping: Organizing merchandise in logical groups such by color or related uses

Handheld: Portable computers designed to collect in-store data

Hands-On Displays: Removing items from packages so customers can handle or use the product before buying it

Hang Tag:

1. Informational tags that hang on merchandise and list quality features, performance specifications, and similar information that helps the consumer reach a buying decision.
2. A hanging price tag used on garments and other merchandise.

Hard Lines: Durable merchandise that includes everything from hardware and appliances to Health and Beauty Accessories

HBA: Acronym for Health and Beauty Accessories or Health and Beauty Aids.

1. Merchandise of over-the-counter medicines and remedies
2. Personal care products, e.g., toothpastes, mouthwashes
3. Hair-care products, e.g., shampoos, setting lotions
4. Body-care products, e.g., body lotion, skin moisturizers
5. Cosmetic products, e.g., perfume, face make ups

Header: Sign for use in a merchandising display with a selling message, product identification, brand name identification, or similar information and placed above displays or shelf sets.

Header Card: Signage used at the very top of a display or fixture

Henry Hanger / Outfitter: A special hanger to display the total outfit or "look" on a 4-way/t-stand/gondola

Hicone: The packaging that holds together multiple units of the same product, such as the plastic rings that hold a six-pack of soda together.

Horizontal Block: A group of one brand or flavor placed on a shelf in a horizontal position. Example: when using this type of set in HBC, all Crest toothpaste would be set across the set instead of putting them on several different shelf heights.

Horizontal Merchandising: Displaying related product items in horizontal sections. Used primarily for merchandise that comes in several types and sizes.

Huddle: Team Meeting

Identifier Sticker: A sticker adhered to product packaging, which communicates that the item is protected against theft or shoplifting.

Impulse Buying: Purchases made by the consumer without any prior planning. A spontaneous purchase made in response to an unexpected urge or external stimulus.

Impulse Displays: Dump bins, movable racks, stack displays, and feature endcaps that promote seasonal items, special buys, advertised specials, new products, closeouts, or price specials in power aisles and other high-traffic areas.

Impulse Merchandise: Items susceptible to spontaneous rather than purposeful purchasing. They are a specific category to convenience goods and tend to be low cost items, e.g., candies, candles.

In and Out Promotions: A short-term promo to induce sales of other products; a once-around feature item not to be restocked as regular shelf merchandise.

In Distribution: Product is authorized to be regularly sold and has been approved for space on the shelf by the chain or store owner; items are on the planograms.

Independent Drug: A store that is not part of a major chain

Indexes: Some stores use this term for a list of stores pertaining to a specific planograms version

Informative Label:

1. A message or affix to merchandise providing data about the item.
2. A label that advised consumers about the care, use, or preparation of a merchandise.

Initial Set: Setting a new product on a shelf/fixture/display

In Line: Product placements within the aisles of the store

In-Line Fixture: The physical permanent fixture, used with pegs or shelves to display product in stock and currently available.

In-Store Demonstration: To increase store sales, an item is demonstrated.

In-Store Lighting: Lighting used not only to make merchandise easily seen and used but also for reducing accidents. Studies have shown that customers tend to examine and handle more merchandise when the lighting is bright than when it is soft.

Inventory: Merchandise in stock and currently available

Inventory Shrink: Reduction in inventory caused primarily by shoplifting and employee theft

Inventory Update: Reporting overstock or out of stock on items

Invoice: Some accounts receive a priced document in their order box. This is given to the account for billing purposes.

Instant Redeemable Coupon: The coupon found on the outside of a package that you can peel off and redeem instantly in the store

Island Display: Island-type display used to hold products in the middle of the store. Is either stacked alone, in a floor display, or on a table.

Item "Cut In": I made space on the shelf and placed a shelf tag and the product, and it is now available for sale, *or* Product was available with space on the shelf and *I* made a shelf tag allowing it to now be sold and reordered.

Item Number: A number used to identify a product assigned by a particular store chain. See *Order/Stock number.*

IVR: Acronym for Interactive Voice Response. It is an electronic reporting system that allows employers to gather store completions in addition to payroll information via the telephone.

Jewel Case: Plastic outer casing/cover for a CD or DVD

J-Hook: A hook so called because of its J shape. Placed on a shelf used to merchandise products.

Jobber: Wholesaler who sells to independent markets and delivers product to the individual store location

Jump Shelf: An additional shelf that will be offset from the other run of shelves

Just In Time (JIT): A replenishment system that reorders product every time the cashier rings up a sale

Kick Plate: Metal plate running along the bottom of the gondola or peg wall from the floor to the base (bottom) shelf. Also known as base plate.

Kiosk:

1. A freestanding display used to provide merchandise and information;
2. A small leased area, booth or cart inside a mall or store or an interactive display; or
3. A terminal giving access to an intranet or to the Internet from inside a store for ordering or checking on merchandise.

Label: Contains price information for the consumer. Labels are placed in the shelf channels to the left of the product or on the front runners for peg hooks unless MOD instructs otherwise.

JUDITH ADKINS-SPEARS

Lead In: The first product a consumer sees from the main aisle. Planograms have lead-in indicators to show which end of the planogram starts near the main aisle.

Lean-Back: A cardboard display where products are placed in the display but are not shipped filled with this product. The displays are constructed by the manufacturer or by the store personnel and then stocked from products on the shelf. Unit usually Leans Back.

Leave Behind: Information Sheet for Store Management

Left Justified: The lining up of labels below the first facing and to the left of the respective product in the channel

Left-to-Right: Display style used for merchandise of different sizes. Smallest sizes are at the upper left of the display; largest sizes are at lower right.

Light Thief: This is the brand display at the very top of the cosmetics displays. It is always referred to as shelf number 1 on the planogram.

Linear Footage: The *total* number of feet devoted to a category using all the shelves in that category. If you are asked to measure the Linear Footage, this is accomplished by adding up the footage of every single shelf in that category together to come up with a grand total.

Line Listing: See *Shelf Report*

Lip-Locked: Refers to product that is stocked on the shelf but cannot be easily removed because it "catches" on the shelf above it

List Price: Manufacturer's price

Live Label: An EAS label in an active state, which will set off the store alarm system if the merchandise is taken past an authorized check point.

LOA: Acronym for Letter of Authorization. This usually describes a job that a client wants to be done in a store or store chain and is presented to management upon entering the store.

Load and Label: The action taken to load product onto a shelf or peg and to place the corresponding store tag or label for that product.

Loss Leader Merchandise: Merchandise sold at or below cost, intended to bring customers into the store.

LRT: See *RMU*

Maintenance: General upkeep of keeping product set to current schematic/planogram with fixtures, displays, shelf clean.

Manufacturer: Producer of products and merchandise that people buy

Mapping: The process of determining locations and adjacencies of departments and merchandise inside a store

Markdown: A reduction in selling price

Mark Ups (M/U): The difference between merchandise cost and the retail price. Also called gross.

Marketing: Marketing is the process of planning and executing the conception, pricing, promotion, and distribution of ideas, goods, and services.

Mass Merchandising: Type of merchandising practices by accounts that display and sell all kinds of merchandise, usually at discount prices.

Mass Merchant: A discount retailer that carries a wide variety of merchandise. I.e., Wal-Mart, Best Buy, Target, Kmart, etc.

Max Shelf Quantity: The reasonable holding capacity on the modular, front checkouts, sidekicks, or any other areas in the store where merchandise is located.

Memos: Details pertinent information concerning stores' activities

Merchandise Islands: Tables or areas stacked with merchandise as a selling floor promotion

Merchandiser: A person representing a manufacturer involved in working with a product at store level

Merchandising: Activity that ensures that merchandise is in the right place, at the right time, in the right quantity, and at the right price.

Midway: *See* Action Alley

Mirrored Image: Most POG read from left to right; unless it specifies "Mirror Image" then it is read backward, from Right to Left. A mirrored image set is required if the set is dependent on the number-one item position lining up with the main aisle or front end of the store.

Mix and Match: Offering the consumer a choice of several different or similar items at a total price, i.e., "Your Choice twelve for $1."

Model Stock: The minimum number of pieces of a reorderable item to be kept in store at all times. Usually based on store volume of fixture fill.

Modular Integrity: See *Proof*

Modular or MOD: Different stores use this term in different ways. It may refer:

1. The permanent or freestanding fixture, used with pegs or shelves to display product OR
2. The planogram of one section of the shelving unit.

Moldings: The outer most edge of the shelf where the shelf tags/labels are to be placed

MSI: See *Order/Stock number*

MSRP: Manufacturers' Suggested Retail Price not to be confused with the retailers' discounted selling price

Multipack: Two or more units attached to each other with the intent to sell as one item

Multiple Pricing: Pricing a single item in units of more than one, i.e., three for 25¢.

Mystery Shop: Store visit requiring merchandiser anonymity in order to evaluate customer service or gather product information in an unbiased manner; form of market research.

Neck Hanger: Tag or POS placed on around the "neck" of the product or peg

960 Unit: Handheld scanner linked to a computer network. The unit will scan the tag or bar code on a product and then you can order, audit, survey, inventory, etc. See *Telzon, RMU.*

Nested: Packaged one within another

New Item: Any item not on the previous planogram/modular that is being introduced to store

New Item Tag: A special tag placed on the shelf molding or peg where there is a new product and the store has not had the opportunity to order yet

New Mod Has Dropped: The phrase used to say the new planogram has been published and is ready to be set

Night Crew: A group of store personnel that work in the store during the late PM hours, usually restocking the shelves

No Tag: The item is "on the shelf" and in the correct location but is missing a shelf tag

NOF: Acronym for Not On File. A bar code or item number that is not in the system.

Nonreplenishable: Product that cannot be reordered from warehouse

Nonsalable: Because of their condition or some other variable, goods that are not offered for sale to the public.

JUDITH ADKINS-SPEARS

Not Authorized: The item is "authorized" for the chain you are in, however, is "not authorized" for the specific store you are in.

Objective Reporting: Reporting facts, not opinions or personal viewpoints.

Off Label Pricing: Special consumer saving marked on the label

On Hand Quantity/Count: The quantity of the item perpetual inventory shows in the system, including on the sales floor, in the backroom and any hidden areas.

On Shelf: This occurs when you enter the store and the product is on the shelf, tagged, and available for sale to the consumer.

Out of Stock (OOS): The product is normally sold in the store but is not available for sale at this time

Open-Date Labeling: Clearly printed, the date marked on merchandise with limited shelf life.

Opening Line: This is a sentence that you may be asked to start a visit with in order to prompt a member of staff

Open Question: This is a question you might be asked by a member of the staff at a branch as part of a visit for which there is an open range of possible responses

Order/Stock Number: An additional number issued to each item carried by a particular chain. This number is used for reordering from the warehouse. Also may be referred to as a MSI, item number, or order code number.

OTC: Acronym for Over the Counter. These are health, beauty care and drug items that do not require a medical prescription for purchase

Outrigger: A rack system that fits over a standard gondola in the sales area

Outsourcing: When a company uses employees or independents from a company other than their own

Over/Under: Two separate types of merchandise placed in one section, divided by shelves, i.e., dry dog food on the bottom shelves and canned dog food on the top shelves

Overlays: A plastic overlay for peg hooks that hold the shelf tag/label

Overhead: The shelf above a section used to hold overstocks or discontinued items. Also called Cap Shelf.

Overstock: Additional stock remaining after the shelf or peg is full to capacity

Pack Out:

1. Putting a shipped order on the shelves.
2. Shelf term referring to the number of units necessary to eliminate out-of-stocks.
3. The total number of packages of an item on a shelf when fully-stocked, shelf capacity, or holding power.

Pack-Size Label Change: New package size or newer labeled product should be placed behind the old

Pad: A designated display area

Pallet: A wooden platform used to ship or stack merchandise on. See also *Stack Base.*

Pallet Displays: When merchandise that arrives on a shipping pallet and is placed on the sales floor while still on the pallet

Pallet Jack: A hydraulic device used to move loaded pallets from one location to another

Pallet Rack: Large industrial sized racks found in backroom/warehouses that are used to stack loaded pallets on

PayPal: An eBay company through which shoppers are paid

PDQ: Acronym for Predetermined Quantity Display. OR Shipper OR Prepack or Sidekick OR Pretty Darn Quick. These displays are called this because they are that fast to set up. They come preloaded with product. Some are either used as clip strips or in sidekicks.

Peg Board: The backboard of a wall or gondola section that has a series of holes (usually one-inch apart) into which peg hooks are inserted to display product

Peg Hooks: Metal or plastic hooks that fit into the pegboard to hold product. When completing a POG that calls for a specific size of a peg hook, the size is determined by length of busable space of the hook.

Pegged: Product that is merchandised on peg hooks, pegboard.

Pegged Merchandise: Product that is merchandised on peg hooks

Pegging: Placement of merchandise on shelf hooks. Items pegged must be carded or have some way of being hung on perfboard display or shelf hook.

Perforated Hardboard: This is tempered hardboard which is predrilled with evenly spaced holes to accept pegs or hooks to support various items, such as tools in a workshop.

Permanent Merchandiser: A permanent fixture within the store that is freestanding

Perpetual Inventory System: System is linked to the POS replenishment system and is used to track movement of inventory from warehouse to store to out the front door as an item is purchased

Persuasive Label: The label, whose primary objective is to attract the consumer to buy the item and not to inform with information

Physical Inventory: Physically counting the individual items in stock

Planogram:

1. A schematic drawing of fixtures that illustrate product placement.

2. Picture or layout plan describing where merchandise is to be placed on fixtures.
3. Also known as Plan-A-Grams, Planograms, POGs, Schematics, or Modulars.
4. Diagram showing where and how merchandise is displayed within the store. It tells store personnel and management where every item is located

Platform: Flat display unit used to display seasonal or bulky merchandise

PO: Purchase order used to ship product to a store

Purchase Order (PO) Number: This number is needed for vendors to order merchandise

POG Profile: Measurements by length and height the spacing between shelves and peg holes

Pole Topper: An upright fixture used in a merchandise display to hold POS signing material

POP:

1. Point of Purchase OR Proof of Purchase.
2. Printed material that draws attention to the product on the shelf or display unit (usually cardboard) or
3. Advertising materials (such as channel strips, shelf talkers, wobblers, premium pads, etc.) placed in the aisle of a store.

Point of Purchase / Point of Sale (POP/POS): Promotional material placed near product shelf or display

Point of sale (POS): Term normally used to describe cash register systems that record transactions or the area of checkout in a retail store

Point-of-sale (POS) System: A computerized system used to track sales through cash registers in the stores

Point-of-sale (POS) Materials: Same as POP materials but placed at the cash register area

Power Wing: This is a larger temporary display that attaches to the side of a fixture

Preassembled Display (PAD): Display with merchandise packed inside the display prior to shipment rather than shipping display and product separately. See *PDQ.*

Preawareness: Sharing promotional material and information with store management to make them aware and excited about an upcoming new release

Preferred Product: Shelves that are located between hip level and eye level

Prepriced: A package label with an existing MSRP placed on the hangtag before shipped to the customer

Preticketing: The product arrives at store level with tickets already on

Price Look-Up or PLU: a number assigned by the retailer as an item's product code. Used typically for the non-UPC-coded products such as produce, fresh bakery goods, and large, hard to scan goods such as charcoal.

Price Point:

1. Retail price of an item.
2. Each shelf location and peg must display the price of the product at that location.
3. In displays or fixtures, items that are grouped by price in one location can be marked with one price point.

Price Tags: Depending on your store could mean one of two different things:

1. The actual price tag that is on the product
2. The Shelf Label.

Private Label: A store's in-house brand

Product Display: An arrangement of a shelf, rack, clip strips, freestanding display, etc., of product

Product Positioning: The way in which a product is characterized to attract consumer interest and purchase.

Product Rotation: The practice of placing new items under or behind older goods that lie on the shelf; purports to ensure the sale of the older products first.

Product Stopper: A small hard plastic or rubber disc that fits on a peg. It is put at the back of the peg behind hanging product, then used to position product at the front of the peg. Gives pegs that "full" appearance that merchandisers want!

Profile: See *Gondola*

Project: A type of service that varies in description and is usually a one-time call, and must be completed within a given time frame.

Project Displays: Merchandise related to a single project displayed with information signs, how-to brochures, and other informative material.

Promotion: Special allowances of discounts offered on products by suppliers

Proof: Audit to check if products on shelf match authorized planogram. Sometimes referred to as checking modular or schematic integrity.

Proof of Purchase: Piece of the package consumers use to prove the product was purchased.

Pull: Remove product. It may go to returns or be destroyed at store level.

Pull and Plug: The action taken to pull existing discontinued product and replace with new product.

Pull Facing: A sample of items to be used into a section. Two pieces of each item should be used. May also be called a One Around.

Punch-Out: Not what you do to difficult store employees! *See Cut-Case.*

Pusher: A fixture component that pushes product to the front of the row.

Questionnaire: The pages of questions which are filled out by the shopper after completing a visit or call.

Racetrack: An aisle that runs around the whole store.

Racetrack Layout: Synonymous with *closed-loop layout.*

Rack: the floor stand for holding goods on shelves, hooks, or in pockets.

Rack Jobber:

1. A limited-service wholesaler that supplies nonfood products to supermarkets, grocery stores, and drug retailers.
2. A wholesaler who maintains stocks of convenience-type merchandise, primarily in supermarkets, drugstores, and other related retail operations. He/she delivers merchandise by vehicle, sets up displays and makes frequent visits to stores and refills the inventory of display items.

Rambler: A six-inch-tall wheeled cart used to transport large amounts of merchandise on and off selling floor

Rat Pack: The hiding of excess stock that is placed elsewhere in the section (usually behind adjacent product)

Rebate: A cash or credit refund offered to customer for purchasing a product

Recall: Product being recalled and returned to distribution center or manufacturer at their request

Receiving: Located in the backroom area where product is processed as it is shipped in

Receiving Desk: The desk where the Receiver works. The Receiver usually works AM shifts.

Regional Manager: Person responsible for a activity within a geographic region of the country

Related Items: Products that are used together

Reorder: Orders placed on all products, up to model stock level, on every visit.

Repack: Overstock that is repacked in boxes (usually banana boxes or similar sized boxes)

Repair Tabs: Plastic tabs that are used to repair damaged holes on hanging product packaging. See *Do Its*.

Replenishment: To fill or make complete again; add a new stock or supply to

Report: Product generated from questionnaire answers and comments, which is sent to the client after data entry and proofreading.

Reps: Field Merchandisers/Representatives

Reserve Stock: Merchandise that is stored in an area inaccessible by customers

Reset: All or part of the sections are disassembled and reassembled according to a new POG, in which many products are moved, facings are increased or decreased, old products are deleted, and new products are cut in.

Retag: Changing old shelf labels with new. This is necessary to update the shelf label information and should always be done if new labels are available.

Retailer: An individual or firm that sells goods and services directly to the consumer

Retrofit:

1. To furnish or affix parts or equipment made available after the time of original manufacture,
2. To modify an existing floor plan or fixtures to new specifications.

Return Authorization: The directive that permits a retailer to return unsold or undamaged merchandise to the manufacturer. This return usually must be accompanied by a **RA number** to process a return.

Return Authorization (RA) Number: Number needed in order to process a return. This number will be supplied to you in your instructions on returning the product. You will then relay the RA number to the claims clerk along with the product.

Return Center: A place that a chain sends back returns to get reimbursed for product

Returns: Product that is authorized to be returned to vendor or warehouse for reimbursement. The product may be damaged, is no longer carried by the store or is excess stock.

Return to Vendor (RTV): The process used to return product

Ribboned: See *Vertical Block*

Riser: Shelves above the shoppable portion of a gondola

RMU:

1. Hand held scanner linked to a computer network, used in Kmart stores; also known as an LRT.
2. The unit will scan the tag or bar code on a product and then you can order, audit, survey, inventory, etc.
3. When connected to a portable printer called a Label Maker you can scan a bar code and print shelf label. *See also Telzon, 960 Unit.*

Rollback: Wal-Mart term for price reduction

Rolling Rack: A semipermanent display fixture on wheels that can be easily moved to different areas of the store

Rolling Steps: Steps with wheels

Rotate Stock:

1. Stock new merchandise behind old merchandise when filling displays.
2. Can also mean replacing old stock with new stock.

Rotation: Putting new product behind any existing product. Dated items: oldest product is placed in front of newer product so the oldest will sell through.

ROTO: Like a circular, a multipage flyer published by retailers for consumers.

Rounder: A circular display rack for large numbers of garments or other goods; can be rotated by the customer for greater convenience and accessibility to the merchandise.

Row Run: (A.k.a. Tag Run) These are the printed labels for every product in a given category

Sales Promotion: Any special activity designed to bring attention to and increase the sales of a product, i.e., Contests, giveaways, celebrity endorsements.

Sales Tag: A preprinted tag that is utilized in front of product that gives sale date title name and UPC (note most common in Circuit City)

Salvage Goods: Goods that are soiled beyond reclamation for purposes of sale and thus usually disposed of by other means

Samples: Free, small packages of product used to introduce the consumer to the product.

Sampling: Putting one item in its designated area to check spacing, arrangement and overall effect before all items are stocked.

Scan Hook: A peg hook that has a label holder at the end where the label is placed and is easily scanned by computer equipment

Scanners: An electronic instrument that reads bar codes and other graphic information found on product packages, coupons, and mailing envelopes.

Scanning:

1. Use of an electronic wand passed over a shelf tag to pick up the item code and relay it to an inventory system.
2. Used at store checkout where product is passed over scanner and price/description is relayed to the cash register.

Scheduler: The person who offers you the assignment

Schematic: Line-art drawing of the planogram, showing how many shelves or peg hooks to use.

Schematic Integrity: See *Proof*

Seasonal Department: A portion of the store given over to goods that are closely related to a specific season, such as a Valentine Day decoration shop.

Seasonal Merchandise: Items so closely identified with a specific season or holiday that they have a very short sales life (e.g., Easter candy and novelties).

Secret Shopper: A merchandiser who samples service or products without the knowledge of the employees and reports the findings to the manufacturer or merchandising company.

Section: The individual fixture units that combine to create an aisle

Segmented Merchandising: Items for sale that were carefully selected to appeal to certain age groups, persons with similar social and economic backgrounds, and so on.

Selling Area: The total floor space given over to selling activities, including aisles, fitting rooms, and adjacent stockrooms.

Sell-Out: To dispose of an entire stock or set of products

SEM / Shelf Label: The label on a POG'd area that shows all information for the product (ie: UPC / date of label / product description / store item number).

Service Activity: Activity performed on the day of service

Service Center: The portion of a store given over to activities such as watch repairs, appliance repairs.

Service Recovery: Dealing effectively with customer complaints, problems, and dissatisfaction.

Service Representative: Person responsible for timely store service and all activities in assigned stores

Set: Refers to the existing way the products are placed when you walk into a store. You will hear "The set includes the such and such product" or "The section is set to planogram."

Set Crew: A team of chain and/or vendor supplied people assigned to a specific store outlet for the purpose of store remodels

Shelf: Any permanent shelving

Shelf Brackets: Metal arms that are inserted into the upright bars on the back of a shelving unit. Shelves are then placed on top of supporting metal brackets.

Shelf Channel: The indented front of the shelf where labels or plastic label strip holders are placed

Shelf Exposure: The number of rows of shelf space a product requires

Shelf Extenders: A tray or display fixture designed to be affixed to the shelf to attract customers' attention and create additional product space

Shelf Fixture: A fixture used to display product on a shelving unit

Shelf Flag: See *Shelf Talker*

Shelf Label:

1. A label/sticker placed on the molding of the shelf identifying product.
2. May also contain description of product size, price, UPC code, ordering code, movement, date tag was printed and store item number.
3. Also sometimes called a Price Tag or Shelf Tag.

Shelf Life: The time identified on the package or label that a certain item can remain in stock or on the shelf before deterioration of a significant nature occurs

Shelf Organizer: Lightweight trays used to hold products on the shelf

Shelf Pack: The inner carton in a master pack

Shelf Profile: Refers to the width of shelves, the distance between them and whether they are straight or inclined.

Shelf Report: A list attached to the POG with full descriptions of the product with a corresponding number of the order they should go on the shelf. It may also include a new and discontinued item listing. Also known as Line Listing.

Shelf Stock: Items available to store customers who remove what they desire form the shelves on which the merchandise are placed

Shelf Strips: An advertising message for shelf stock, affixed to the shelf molding. Also known as Channel Strips.

Shelf Tag: Label that identifies product on shelf

Shelf Talker: A small sign that attaches to the molding of the shelf and points out sale, product features or price. Also known as Bean Flips.

Shelving Unit: The physical permanent fixture used with pegs or shelves to display product. A general term describing Gondolas, Side Counters, In-Line fixtures, and Modulars.

Shipper Pack: A prepackaged display carton, which can be opened up, assembled and placed directly on the sales floor or counter. Also called Prepack or Self-Shipper.

Showcase: A glass or see through display unit containing merchandise that is not easily accessible to customers. Used to prevent product damage or theft.

Shrink: The dollar difference in what a store counts at inventory and what it has on paper

Shroud: A cardboard advertisement that slips over a fixture/pole or security gates in the store

Side Counter: The physical permanent fixture, used with pegs or shelves to display product.

Side Kick: A small product display that hangs on the side of an endcap, a.k.a. Power Wing

Side Rack: See *Side Kick*

Side Stack: Displays placed along the side of a grocery aisle

Sign In For (SIF): Terminology used when on a remodel or an attend and assist assignment representing a client. Usually you are asked to sign in on a list of attending vendors.

Signage:

1. Signs that are used on fixtures and can be removed or replaced.

2. These signs highlight an item by attracting the customer's attention to its low price, new item, product information, etc.

605 Clerk: See *Claims Clerk*

Size Class: A store is classified by size (square footage) which determines the product mix and section size. Each department also has a class size that is determined by sales volume.

Size Lining: Items, mostly apparel, grouped together in the store by size rather than by price or by lifestyle.

Stock-Keeping Unit (SKU):

1. Refers to each single item carried by a retailer.
2. Every size, every style, and every item having its own vender number has a stock-keeping unit with its own SKU number.
3. Some SKU's have more than one facing.
4. Each SKU is associated with a different product on a planogram (POG) and is a number assigned by the retailer to keep track of the type, color, and size of a product.
5. Some stores refer to the UPC number as the SKU.
6. See also Order/Stock number and UPC number.

Sky Deck: Same as Riser

Sky Hook Peg: Fastback metal peg with label holder attached. Front-runner is not used

Skyline: The tallest height that a product can be placed

Slap and Stick: This occurs when the company only wants you to peel the old label from the fixture and "Slap the new one up and Stick it" on.

Slatwall: The back wall section of an aisle that holds merchandise up on slat pegs

Slip Sleeve: A paper sleeve casing/cover for video product

Snap Railing: A rail with sliding pegs attached

Softlines: Ready-to-wear clothing, piece goods, linens, towels, and small fashion accessories.

Sold Rhrough, Sold Out: Usually refers to a special promotional item that is nonreplenishable

Specialty Retailer: A retail outlet that concentrates its merchandising efforts in a particular category of items within that category. I.e., Toys "R" Us, Ace Hardware

Spinner Rack: A fixture that rotates around for the customer to view product

Spine: Display items like books in a library

Split or Wraparound Sections: This simply means that the section is split into two sections, one on one side of the gondola/aisle and the other wrapping around to the other side.

Split-Rounder: An apparel display fixture composed of two hemispheres, one elevated above the other for greater 360-degree visibility.

Spoils or Spoilage: Merchandise found to be defective

Spoils Recovery: A place that a chain sends back spoils to, to get reimbursed by the manufacturer or vendor of that product.

Stack Base: A four-by-four-inch wooden or rubber square used in Action Alley to display merchandise

Stickering: The action taken to place stickers on product. These may include coupons, rebate offers, product updates or corrections of info on packaging.

Stickers: Items that have not been purchased after a reasonable time and occupy space considered important for better-selling items

Stock:

1. Merchandise held for sale (e.g., inventory)
2. Material in inventory

Stock Depth: Merchandise determined to be needed to maintain assortments without too many lost sales because of an out-of-stock situation

Stock Rotation: Putting new incoming products behind those of the same kind already on the shelf so that inventory remains fresh

Stock Turnover: A measure for determining how quickly merchandise is being sold

Stockout: When a shelf is empty where a particular product is supposed to be placed; denotes you are out of stock on this item.

Stocking Crew: See *Night Crew*

Store Door Delivery: See *Direct Store Delivery*

Style Numbers: Help to identify the product located on the price tags

Subcontracting: Outsourcing rep labor

SuperCenter: Wal-Mart's name for their Super Stores

SuperStore: A larger than average supermarket or discounter. Example: Target Superstore, Wal-Mart SuperCenter.

Surge: Expanded or increased need for a reset due to a new item initiative

Surge Blitz: See *Blitz*

Surveys: Questionnaire that collects information requested by customer/client

Swell Allowance: A predetermined amount to be deducted from the face of an invoice to a wholesaler or a retailer, intended to cover estimated spoilage of age sensitive products.

Syndicated: Working with a variety of accounts/clients

T-Stands:

1. Basic apparel fixtures with posts topped by cross bars
2. A display frame just inside the door. It usually has that week's sale paper tacked on it.

Table Tent: A cardboard or plastic sign folded like a tent that sits on a tabletop or counter to advertise in an item

Tagged: This item was a VOID when I entered the store. I was able to make space for the item on the shelf and place the tag, but no product is currently available for sale.

Tag Run: A print out of all labels needed for a specific category in the store. Also known as a "Row run."

Tag Up: Shelf tag or label in place on a shelf

Tagged: You were able to make space for the product on the shelf and place a shelf tag, but no product is currently available for sale to the consumer.

Take Stock: To make an inventory of items on hand

Talking Stick: This is similar to a metal clip strip, but it stands vertically on a counter.

Target Time: The company's anticipated length time it will take for the merchandiser to complete a project

Tear Off Pads: Sheets of paper that can be removed one at a time by the consumer. They give information about the product that they are placed near.

Telzon: Hand held tracking unit used to order and track store inventory

Temporary Merchandiser: Cardboard freestanding display vehicle sent in with a new release or promotion item used to display the product

Testers: Samples of product not for sale but made available to the customer to "test" (look, touch, feel, try on, etc.).

Test Market: A process whereby a manufacturer introduces and markets a product or program in a controlled geographical area

Tether: A cable that connects one piece of a display to another piece of the display

Tie-In Sales: The cooperation at retail in promoting a product during a consumer advertising period conducted by the manufacturer, uniform promotion; follow-through at the point of sale.

Territory Manager (TM): Another name for a merchandiser

Top Stock: Overstock that is placed in the overheads

Totes: Plastic boxes that hold product shipped from warehouse, a.k.a. Trays

Traffic Flow: The pattern of planned traffic movement of consumers through a department or the store (usually designed to take consumers past the high-profit items or departments)

Traited: A particular product that the store is authorized to carry is said to be "traited for the store"

Trays: See *Totes*

Tray Pack: A point-of-purchase display where the top of the case of goods can be opened and folded back so that the case actually becomes a display tray that is readily placed on a shelf or counter in the store

Tri-Level Round: An apparel fixture with three face-out arms

Tubs: See *Totes*

Turns: The number of times a product completes the cycle of moving through a warehouse or retail store, i.e., The number of times a warehouse is completely rotated.

Understock: Product that cannot be displayed on fixtures; See also *Backstock*.

Universal Product Code (UPC): Standard for encoding a set of lines and spaces that can be scanned and interpreted into numbers to identify a product

UPC Number:

1. A sequence of numbers and bar code on the back of each product.
2. It is located with the bar code on the product and on the shelf label.
3. Some stores refer to the UPC number as the SKU OR
4. Stores use it as their order/stock number.

UPC Office: The office or clerk responsible for scanning all items in the store

Upright Bars: The upright bars that are on the back wall of a shelving unit. Shelves are placed upon extending shelf brackets that are inserted into the upright bars

Upright Freezer: Standing freezer case with glass doors

Variety: See *General Merchandise*

Vendor: Person or company providing merchandise or service to a retail store

Vendors' Log: Book and/or sheets used by retailers to identify vendors/visitors in their stores.

Vertical: Top to bottom striping of a product

Vertical Block:

1. A group of one brand placed on two or more shelves directly above and below each other in the same locations on each shelf.

2. Also referred to as Ribboned or just called a block.

Vertical Merchandising: Displaying related product categories in vertical sections. Largest items displayed on lower shelves.

Vignette: A display that simulates a product in actual use

Visual Merchandising: Arranging items for display, also known as Visual Presentation.

Visible Shrinkage: Stock shortage because of wear and tear or breakage of items

Vendor-Managed Inventory (VMI): When a company keeps a record of the store's inventory and automatically ships to sales and credits

VOID: The item is authorized to be on the shelf, but there is no shelf space, no shelf tag, and no product available for the consumer to purchase.

Volume-Producing Item: An item chosen by Department Managers or higher management that is featured to produce sales and raise the gross

Voice-Response Unit (VRU): The system for reps to report their daily work via touchtone phone

Wall Area: The area around the perimeter of the store used to display merchandise on peg, shelf, fixtures, etc.

Wallpaper: This paper covers the pegboard before pegs are inserted. It usually has holes where the pegs are to be placed. Wallpaper is sometimes referred to as a template.

Warehouse: Where suppliers store product until a retailer places an order. Items are ordered from the hand held scanner and are shipped directly from the warehouse.

Well: Open stocking under the shelving area on the base of a deli case

Wing Display: A display that flanks or attaches to the side of an endcap

Wobbler: A type of shelf talker that when attached to the shelf strip actually wobbles or waves in the air

Zero Out: Term for correcting the inventory that automatically generates an order

Zone: General upkeep of keeping product set to current schematic/planogram

Zone Pricing: A pricing structure made up of different levels. Price levels are based on price comparisons with major competitors, area, etc.

JUDITH ADKINS-SPEARS

INDEX

JUDITH ADKINS-SPEARS

gross floor space, 185
grouping, 74, 173, 185

H

handheld, 143, 185
on hand quantity/count, 193
hands-on displays, 185
hang tag, 185
hard lines, 185
HBA (Health and Beauty Accessories/
    Health and Beauty Aids), 185
HBC, 184, 186
header, 63, 120, 144, 185
header card, 185
Henry Hanger/Outfitter, 185
hicone, 186
horizontal block, 186
horizontal merchandising, 186
How to Win Friends and Influence People
    (Carnagie), 125
huddle, 186

I

identifier sticker, 186
impulse buying, 186
impulse displays, 186
impulse merchandise, 186
independent drug, 186
indexes, 187
informative label, 187
initial set, 187
in-line fixture, 187
instant redeemable coupon, 187
in-store demonstration, 187
in-store lighting, 187
inventory, 22, 36, 187
inventory shrink, 187
inventory update, 187
invoice, 139-40, 187
island display, 73, 144, 187
item "cut in," 188
item number, 49, 143, 180, 188
IVR (Interactive Voice Response), 89, 188

J

jewel case, 188
J-Hook, 61, 82, 143, 188
JIT (Just In Time), 188
jobber, 188, 199
JRQ (Job Review Questionnaire), 40
jump shelf, 188

K

kick plate, 188
kiosk, 188

L

label, 37, 39, 45-46, 49-51, 60, 80, 83,
    90, 143, 178, 187-88, 193, 195,
    197-98, 201, 205
lead in, 189
lean-back, 189
leave behind, 189
left justified, 189
left-to-right, 189
light thief, 189
in line, 187
linear footage, 189
line listing, 189, 205. *See also* shelf report
lip-locked, 189
list price, 189
live label, 189
LOA (Letter of Authorization), 189
load and label, 37, 190
loss leader merchandise, 190
LRT, 51, 143, 190, 201. *See also* RMU

M

maintenance, 133
manufacturer, 14, 18, 22, 25, 27, 47-49,
    62, 64, 66, 190
mapping, 190
markdown, 175, 190
marketing, 190
mass merchandising, 190
mass merchant, 190
max shelf quantity, 190
memos, 190

system, 196

power wing, 183, 197. *See also* side kick

preawareness, 197

preferred product, 197

prepriced, 197

preticketing, 197

price look-up, 197

price point, 197

price tags, 85, 185, 197

private label, 198

product display, 198

product positioning, 198

product rotation, 198

product stopper, 198

project, 198

project displays, 198

promotion, 198

proof, 191, 198. *See also* schematic integrity

proof of purchase, 198

pull, 52, 84, 198

pull and plug, 37, 198

pull facing, 199

punch-out, 199

pusher, 199

Q

questionnaire, 40, 168, 199, 209

R

RA (return authorization) number, 88, 201

racetrack, 199

racetrack layout, 174, 199. *See also* closed-loop layout

rack, 70, 144, 168, 199

rack jobber, 199

rambler, 199

rat pack, 199

rebate, 30, 199

recall, 199

receiving, 200

  desk, 200

regional manager, 200

related items, 200

reorder, 200

repack, 200

repair tabs, 85, 179, 200. *See also* Do ITs

replenishment, 169, 200

report, 200

reps, 200

reserve stock, 200

reset, 38, 44, 80, 90-91, 200

retag, 36, 200

retailer, 75, 200

retrofit, 201

return center, 201

returns, 83, 201

ribboned, 201. *See also* vertical block

riser, 53, 60, 143, 207. *See also* sky deck

RMU, 51, 143, 201. *See also* LRT

rollback, 171, 201

rolling rack, 69, 144

rolling steps, 202

rotate stock, 202

rotation, 202

ROTO, 202

rounder, 202

row run, 202. *See also* tag run

RTV (return to vendor), 201

S

sales promotion, 202

sales tag, 202

salvage goods, 202

samples, 202

sampling, 202

scan hook, 203

scanners, 203

scheduler, 203

schematic, 36, 74-75, 203. *See also* POG (planogram)

schematic integrity, 203. *See also* proof

seasonal department, 203

seasonal merchandise, 203

secret shopper, 203

section, 203

segmented merchandising, 203

selling area, 204

sell-out, 204

T

table tent, 63, 210
Tagged, 210
tag run, 51, 202, 210. *See also* row run
tag up, 210
take stock, 210
talking stick, 210
target time, 210
tear off pads, 210
Telzon, 210
temporary merchandiser, 211
testers, 211
test market, 211
tether, 211
tie-in sales, 211
TM (territory manager), 211
top stock, 211
totes, 93, 211. *See also* trays
traffic flow, 76
traited, 169. *See also* ASI (Authorized
        Stock Item)
tray pack, 211
trays, 144. *See also* totes
tri-level round, 211
T-Stands, 210
tubs, 211
turns, 27, 212

U

understock, 212
UPC (Universal Product Code), 47-52,
        87, 143, 170, 173, 180, 197, 202,
        205, 207, 212
    number, 47-51, 87, 143, 207, 212
    office, 212

upright bars, 143, 212
upright freezer, 212

V

variety, 212. *See also* GM (general
        merchandise)
vendor, 22
vendors' log, 39-40, 88, 104, 212
vertical, 212-13
    block, 212
    merchandising, 213
vignette, 71, 213
visible shrinkage, 213
visual merchandising, 213
VMI (Vendor-Managed Inventory), 213
VOID, 213
volume-producing item, 213
VRU (Voice-Response Unit), 213

W

wall area, 213
wallpaper, 12, 213
warehouse, 37, 49, 83, 213
well, 213
wing display, 213
wobbler, 214

Z

zero out, 214
zone, 52, 214
    pricing, 214

ABOUT THE AUTHOR

Judith Adkins-Spears, the author of this book, has been a successful merchandiser and mystery shopper for many years. She has the Silver and Gold MSPA certifications, Undercover Video Specialist certification, and Guide to Food Safety Certification.

She was previously a teacher at a business college, a high school, and a middle school. In the field of education, she was awarded much recognition: Southern Business Education Association - Professional Development Award; Kentucky College of Business -Excellence in Teaching Award; Phi Beta Lambda, Inc. – National Fall Leadership Conference; Kentucky Academic Association Official –Governor's Cup Competition. She was chosen to represent the KBEA in a leadership training course at their National Conference.

Judith also belongs to the following professional organizations: Phi Eta Sigma Honor Society - Pikeville College - Founding Member; National Association of Professional Women (NAPW); National Organization for Women (NOW); American Association of Retired People (AARP); Retired Pike County Educators Association; and Retired Kentucky Educators Association. In the past she belonged to the Pike County Educators Association; Kentucky Educators Association; National Educators Association; Kentucky Business Educators Association –Executive Committee; and National Business Educators Association.

Judith also received one of distinguished recognition. Governor Paul Patton awarded her a Kentucky Colonel Membership in recognition for donating her time for four years to the Pikeville College Women's Basketball team as their official scorebook keeper, which included traveling with the team all over the United States.

Working for various merchandising and mystery shopping companies at store level, she has come to enjoy the flexibility this work offers. She finds her reward in encouraging others and contributing to their success. A strong working knowledge of the trade and a sincere desire to help, uniquely qualifies her to teach you to "walk the walk, talk the talk," and prepare you for an exciting and rewarding career.

Judith has been married 42 years, has two grown children and three grandchildren. She makes her home in Eastern Kentucky.

JUDITH ADKINS-SPEARS

Made in the USA
Lexington, KY
10 November 2011